QUEEN ELIZABETH I
BOOK OF DAYS

This book belongs to:

____

____

____

TUDOR TIMES

THE ORIGIN OF BOOKS OF HOURS

During the late Middle Ages and the Renaissance period, one of the most coveted items a literate person could own was the Book of Hours.

Books of Hours were designed to aid lay people in the practice of their religion, by collecting biblical texts, prayers and elements of the liturgy for them to read throughout the day, emulating the 'Hours' or regular services of the religious life.

By the late fifteenth century, Books of Hours were so popular that they were produced en masse. Higher up the social scale, they were individually commissioned, frequently as a bride-gift from husband to wife, and the level of decoration, the number of colours used in the illumination, and the quantity of gold, silver or expensive lapis blue used, depended on what the purchaser could afford.

Books of Hours were personal items, used to record important family events, for example, the entry in 1489, by Lady Margaret Beaufort, mother of King Henry VII, of a note recording the birth of her granddaughter. Friends or lovers might write verses to each other on their pages, an example being a loving exchange between Elizabeth I's parents,

King Henry VIII and Anne Boleyn.

The Reformation led to a decline in the popularity of Books of Hours in Protestant countries, and in England, by the end of Elizabeth's reign, they had been replaced by the family Bible, where births, marriages and deaths were recorded. Almanacs also increased in popularity, combining the calendrical function alongside information about astronomical phenomena, astrological predictions, and dates for undertaking agricultural tasks.

QUEEN ELIZABETH I BOOK OF DAYS

We cannot, alas, reproduce the extraordinary beauty of the original Books of Hours or the complex astrological predictions of almanacs, but in the *Queen Elizabeth I Book of Days*, we have sought to combine some of the functions of the originals in an attractive contemporary format. Our Book of Days is a perpetual calendar, which allows you to enter the events most important to you, your friends and family, and preserve them indefinitely, untrammelled by the days of the week or the year.

The observation of feast and saints' days declined in the latter half of the sixteenth century, so only those days recognised by the Elizabethan church are recorded. For each day of the year, we have highlighted an event related to Queen Elizabeth, either political or personal, expanded in an index-entry. After an overview of Elizabeth's life, each month has a section on an event, and a description of a place important to the queen.

Elizabeth I's signature.

'SEMPER EADEM'
ELIZABETH I

Queen Elizabeth's speech to her last Parliament.

THE LIFE OF ELIZABETH I

Henry VIII and Anne Boleyn confidently expected that their first child would be a son, justifying the break with Rome that had enabled them to marry.

The birth of a daughter, Elizabeth, on 7th September 1533, was therefore disappointing, but the royal couple took comfort in her health.

In 1534, the Act of Succession proclaimed Elizabeth as heir to the kingdom and for the first two and a half years of her life she was petted and indulged. This halcyon period ended when Queen Anne was executed for treason. In the Act of Succession that followed, Elizabeth was branded illegitimate.

Elizabeth's education encompassed Latin, Greek, French, Italian, history, philosophy and mathematics as well as courtly accomplishments. In 1543, Henry VIII married his sixth wife, Katherine Parr, an intelligent and mentally stimulating companion, who greatly influenced Elizabeth.

At Henry's death in January 1547, Elizabeth became second in line to the throne, after her half-siblings, Edward and Mary. The widowed Queen Katherine married Sir Thomas Seymour, who was soon treating Elizabeth in a way that went beyond the teasing of an affectionate step-father and began to look like sexual advances. Elizabeth, aged 14, became embroiled in a dangerous game of flirtation. Katherine tried to defuse the situation by joining in the romps, but the matter went too far, and the mortified and repentant Elizabeth was sent away.

After Katherine's death in childbirth, Seymour put out feelers to see if Elizabeth would be amenable to marriage. Too astute to commit herself, Elizabeth was careful to do nothing that could savour of treason. Seymour was executed in 1549, but despite repeated questioning, no evidence of treason could be found against Elizabeth.

Keen to play down the Seymour scandal, Elizabeth presented herself as the ideal Protestant virgin – plainly dressed, carrying a prayer book, spending her time at her studies, and embracing the religious changes introduced in Edward VI's reign, which turned English official worship from Catholic to Protestant.

In July 1553, on the death of Edward, there was an attempt to subvert the Act of Succession of 1544, bypassing Mary and Elizabeth to install their cousin, Lady Jane Grey, on the throne. Elizabeth did nothing, but waited for events to unfold, a strategy that proved successful and that she continued to follow, seldom making decisions until forced. Mary triumphed, and Elizabeth took part in the new queen's jubilant entry into London. Mary acknowledged Elizabeth as her sister, and there was no immediate pressure to conform to the Catholic practice that Mary reintroduced. But Elizabeth's position was soon threatened by Mary's marriage to Philip of Spain. Any child born of the marriage would displace Elizabeth in the succession.

To prevent Mary's marriage and replace her with Elizabeth was the purpose of a rebellion in 1554, led by Sir Thomas Wyatt. Wyatt was defeated, but Elizabeth was suspected of involvement and sent first to the Tower of London, then to Woodstock, under house arrest.

Gradually the restrictions on her were relaxed, and Elizabeth was permitted to return to court. Papal Supremacy had been restored, the heresy laws re-implemented, and everyone was obliged to conform to traditional Catholic practice. Elizabeth did so, but hinted that she was not convinced – having coughing fits at inopportune moments during the Mass. Nevertheless, her brother-in-law, King Philip, was eager to maintain good relations, preferring the prospect of Elizabeth inheriting the English crown, over the alternative heir, Mary, Queen of Scots, who, although Catholic, was pro-French, which he considered to be worse than Protestantism.

On Mary's death in November 1558, Elizabeth was proclaimed queen. Her first actions were to appoint Lord Robert Dudley as her Master of Horse, and Sir William Cecil as her Secretary.

The issues that faced the new queen were religion, foreign relations, and marriage. Religion was dealt with first. Parliament was called, and papal authority again rejected. Elizabeth was named as Supreme Governor of the Church in England. Next, the form of worship was discussed. Elizabeth herself leant towards the form of the moderate Book of Common Prayer of 1549. But many of the Catholic bishops had resigned and there was an influx of more radical Protestants, who had returned from exile in Geneva, determined to influence Elizabeth. By their careful management, the Catholic majority in the Lords was circumvented and conformity to the slightly moderated Book of Common Prayer of 1552 was instituted, although many of the ceremonies and ornaments of the old faith were retained. This religious settlement, which the radicals thought was just a staging post, was defended by Elizabeth to her dying day. There would be no further reform.

The next point was foreign relations. The 1559 Treaty of Cateau-Cambrésis included England in Spain's peace with France, but with Elizabeth cool towards him, Philip had little incentive to pursue the recovery of Calais. Nevertheless, for many years Elizabeth hoped to regain French territory, and relations with that country remained strained, especially as the Auld Alliance between Scotland and France had culminated in the marriage of Mary of Scotland to François of France. The young Queen Mary had been directed by her father-in-law, Henri II, to quarter the arms of England with her own – signalling her claim to be the rightful queen. Simultaneously, the Scottish Protestant Lords of the Congregation sought Elizabeth's help against the Catholic regent, Marie of Guise. Elizabeth was in a quandary. She was being pushed by Cecil to help the Lords, but did not want to undermine another sovereign. Eventually, she gave secret assistance, and the Lords triumphed. The resulting Treaty of Greenwich acknowledged Elizabeth as Queen of England, although in France Queen Mary refused to ratify the treaty.

The question of marriage was Elizabeth's third problem. In hindsight, her eventual non-marriage seems a wise policy, but it was probably not her fixed intention at the time, and everybody assumed that she ought to marry, although her ministers could not agree on a suitable spouse. Her first suitor was Philip, keen to maintain the Anglo-Spanish alliance. Not choosing to quarrel, Elizabeth let him think she would consider it. Other possible suitors were the sons of the Emperor Ferdinand, the King of

Sweden, and the younger sons of France.

Over the following 25 years, Elizabeth considered marrying first one, then another, of these men but nothing was ever decided. Personally, she was deeply enamoured of Robert Dudley, but he was not only the son of an executed traitor, but also already married. Their relationship caused scandal across Europe, intensified in 1560 when Lady Dudley was found dead at the bottom of a staircase. Dudley was exonerated in the investigation she ordered, but Elizabeth could never marry him.

In 1568, Mary, Queen of Scots arrived in England as a fugitive, deposed by her Lords. Elizabeth was appalled. She needed to reconcile her duty to her cousin and to sovereigns everywhere by supporting Mary, but she did not want the Protestant Reformation undone in Scotland, nor did she wish to give support to a woman whom the majority of her own subjects believed to be her own rightful heir, and whom some thought should be queen already.

Mary was held in confinement whilst Elizabeth pondered. Within a year, the earls of Northumberland and Westmorland led the Rising of the North with the aim of enthroning Mary and restoring the Mass – the last gasp of Catholic, feudal England. The earls were defeated, but Elizabeth became less tolerant of Catholic dissent. The fines for failing to attend the Anglican service were raised from a nominal amount to sums that forced all but the richest to conform.

There were religious problems elsewhere too – the Netherlands were in revolt against Philip of Spain and Elizabeth was being called on to support fellow Protestants. Despite the urging of her government, Elizabeth was reluctant to embroil her kingdom. Nevertheless, throughout the 1570s and early 1580s, England gave the Netherlands limited support. The French were also involved, leading to Elizabeth's last flirtation with marriage, with the French king's brother, the Duke of Anjou.

Meanwhile, plots in favour of Mary, Queen of Scots sprang up – some certainly encouraged, if not instigated, by the agents provocateurs of Sir Francis Walsingham, one of Elizabeth's most radically Protestant ministers, whose spy network reached into every corner of the kingdom. Eventually, Mary received a letter outlining a plot to assassinate Elizabeth. She did not negate the plan in her response, which gave Walsingham and Cecil the opportunity to have her tried for treason. Mary was found guilty, but Elizabeth hesitated to have her executed. Eventually, the deed was done, and this, together with her support for his Netherlandish rebels, and the actions of English shipping in harassing the Spanish fleet, led Philip

of Spain to declare open war. In 1588 he sent an armada to conquer England. It was defeated, through a combination of foul weather and excellent English seamanship. This was the high-water mark of Elizabeth's reign. Her image as Gloriana, safeguarding Protestant England was forever enshrined in English memory. Bolstering this was the expansion of exploration in the Americas and a flowering of literature and language.

As the 1590s unfolded, there were new problems: poor harvests, the clamour of the Puritans for further religious reform, complaints about financial corruption and continuing war with Spain. Religious division in Ireland erupted in a major insurrection in 1594, led by the Earl of Tyrone. Elizabeth sent her favourite, Robert, 2nd Earl of Essex, to subdue it. The resulting bloody and brutal conflict had long-term implications. Essex himself became embroiled in a plot which ended in his execution.

After the death of Essex in 1601, Elizabeth was exhausted and depressed. She refused to name an heir, although she had been corresponding for many years with James VI of Scotland. In early 1603, she fell into melancholy, refusing to eat or to go to bed, and died on 24th March.

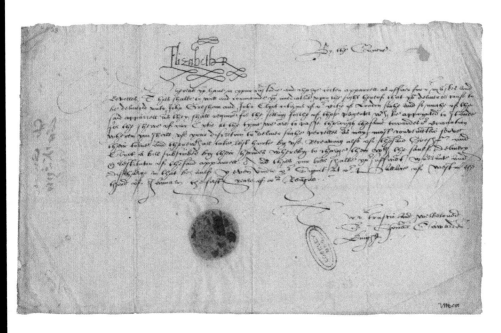

Warrant with sign-manual and signet directing Cawarden to deliver to John Gresham and John Elyot, citizens of London, apparrel required for setting forth a pageant for the queen's coronation. Printed in HMC, 1879.

SONNET

Elizabeth was intellectually, as well as politically, accomplished, writing prayers and sonnets. This sonnet is thought to have been written after she finally declined to marry François, Duke of Anjou.

On Monsieur's Departure

I grieve and dare not show my discontent,
I love and yet am forced to seem to hate,
I do, yet dare not say I ever meant,
I seem stark mute but inwardly do prate.
I am and not, I freeze and yet am burned,
Since from myself another self I turned.

My care is like my shadow in the sun,
Follows me flying, flies when I pursue it,
Stands and lies by me, doth what I have done.
His too familiar care doth make me rue it.
No means I find to rid him from my breast,
Till by the end of things it be supprest.

Some gentler passion slide into my mind,
For I am soft and made of melting snow;
Or be more cruel, love, and so be kind.
Let me or float or sink, be high or low.
Or let me live with some more sweet content,
Or die and so forget what love e'er meant.

FACTS ABOUT ELIZABETH I

1. Elizabeth liked to give her favourite male courtiers nicknames. Sir William Cecil was her 'Spirit', Sir Francis Walsingham her 'Moor', Lord Robert Dudley her 'Eyes' and Sir Christopher Hatton her eye 'Lids'.

2. Amongst her collections of objets d'art was a walking stick made from what was believed to be a unicorn's horn.

3. Elizabeth's bathroom at Windsor had running water, and the walls and ceiling were lined with mirrors.

4. Elizabeth had a strong sense of smell, surrounding herself with flowers and perfumes. She once reprimanded a courtier with the words 'Tush, Man, your boots stink!'

5. The Elector of Saxony gave Elizabeth a backgammon set in which each of the pieces was decorated with pictures of kings and queens, overlaid with crystal, and a board made of ebony and ivory, set with jewels.

6. Elizabeth also had a silver chess set.

7. Elizabeth's fool, Monarcho, was so renowned that Shakespeare included him as a character in *Love's Labour's Lost*.

8. Elizabeth employed the famous mathematician, seer, and alchemist Dr John Dee, and had a suite of rooms at Hampton Court furnished with alchemical equipment for him.

9. Every six months, Elizabeth's pin-supplier, Robert Carles, would deliver around 24,000 pins of different sizes for fastening her apparel.

10. Ivan the Terrible, Tsar of Russia, sent Elizabeth four timbers of sable, lynx and ermine furs.

11. In 1561, Elizabeth received one of the first known pairs of knitted silk stockings, which she vastly preferred to the old cloth ones.

12. Elizabeth is alleged to have broken the finger of one of her maids-of-honour by throwing a hairbrush at her.

PERSONAL DETAILS

Name

Surname

Home address

Telephone

Mobile

E-mail

Date of birth

Place of birth

Website

Wi-Fi

Login

Home Wi-Fi

Login

Family doctor	Dentist
Address	Address
Telephone	Telephone
Blood group	
Allergies	
Vaccinations	
Passport No	
Valid until	
Visa	
Expiry date	
Driving licence	
Expiry date	

YEAR PLANNER

January

February

March

April

May

June

July

August

September

October

November

December

MONTH PLANNER

January

1 Elizabeth presented her own translation of *Mirror of a Sinful Soul* to Katherine Parr (1544)

2 Elizabeth wrote to Edward VI, explaining her long absence from court as due to sickness (1552)

3 Elizabeth approved Richard Fletcher's promotion from Bishop of Worcester to Bishop of London (1595)

4 Roger Ascham, Elizabeth's tutor, was buried (1569)

5 Catherine de' Medici, regent to three French kings, died (1589)

6 Jean de Simier arrived from France to negotiate a marriage between François, Duke of Anjou and Elizabeth (1579)

7 Troops of Duke of Anjou, Elizabeth's suitor, defeated in attempt to take Antwerp (1583)

8 Elizabeth's ships left Portsmouth to attack Newhaven, in France (1563)

9 Michael Moody confessed to conspiring to assassinate Elizabeth (1587)

10 Elizabeth's government ordered arrest of all Jesuits (1581)

11 Merchants of the Staple requested compensation for their goods seized in the Netherlands (1569)

12 Elizabeth travelled by barge from Whitehall to Tower of London to prepare for her coronation (1559)

13 Elizabeth issued a licence to Southampton to hold three fairs a year (1599)

14 Elizabeth processed from Tower of London to Westminster on eve of her coronation (1559)

15 Elizabeth crowned Queen of England (1559)

16 Parliament demanded the execution of Mary, Queen of Scots (1581)

17 Elizabeth wrote to Duke of Anjou (1580)

18 Henry VII of England married Elizabeth of York (1486)

19 Elizabeth began a three-day visit to Earl of Nottingham at Chelsea, Middlesex (1600)

20 Elizabeth wrote to Ottoman Sultan, Mahumet (1601)

21 Bill of Attainder passed against Katheryn Howard, Henry VIII's fifth wife (1542)

22 Elizabeth granted musicians Thomas Tallis and William Byrd a 25-year monopoly to print music (1575)

23 Elizabeth officially opened the Royal Exchange in London (1571)

24 Thomas Boleyn, Earl of Wiltshire and of Ormond, appointed Lord Privy Seal (1530)

25 Elizabeth's first Parliament opened (1559)

26 Thomas Howard, 4th Duke of Norfolk, degraded from Order of the Garter (1572)

27 Francis Drake, courtier and explorer, died in the harbour at Porto Bello (1596)

28 Henry VII of England was born (1457)
Henry VIII of England died (1547)

29 Edward VI and Elizabeth were told of Henry VIII's death (1547)

30 Elizabeth began a three-day visit to The Strand in London, hosted by Sir Robert Cecil (1593)

31 Commission convened to investigate relationship between Earl of Hertford and queen's cousin, Lady Katherine Grey (1562)

Birthdays	Anniversaries	Reminders	Projects

Gardening	Events	Occasions	Festivals

ELIZABETH'S CORONATION PROCESSION

The 15th January 1559 was selected as the most propitious date for Elizabeth's coronation. Three days before, she sailed from Westminster to the Tower. Entering its precincts, she declared that *'Some people have fallen from being Princes of this land, to be prisoners in this place. I am raised from a prisoner in this place to be a Prince of this land. That dejection was a work of God's justice; this advancement is a work of his mercy.'*

On 14th January she departed for Westminster, preceded by trumpeters and heralds. Along the route were tableaux, illustrating London's views on how Elizabeth should govern. The first was at the Eagle in Gracechurch Street and comprised a triumphal arch over a tiered stage. At the foot, actors played the queen's grandparents, Henry VII and Elizabeth of York, from whom branches of red and white roses emerged to entwine into a platform for Elizabeth's parents, Henry VIII and Anne Boleyn. Above was a throne, with an actor representing Elizabeth, crowned and holding a sceptre.

The next pageant showed Elizabeth in the 'Seat of Worthy Governance', supported by virtues – Pure Religion, Love of Subjects, Wisdom and Justice, trampling vices: Superstition, Rebellion, Folly and Bribery.

At Cheapside, the Aldermen presented a purse of gold. Elizabeth responded,

'...I will be as good unto you as ever queen was to her people. No will in me can lack, neither do I trust shall lack any power. And persuade yourselves, that for the safety and quietness of you all, I will not spare, if need be, to spend my blood.'

The third tableau comprised two hills with landscape scenes, one a barren and withered 'Decayed Commonwealth', the other, 'fair, fresh and beautiful', showing a 'Flourishing Commonwealth'. Father Time led forth his daughter, Truth, who proffered an English Bible, which Elizabeth kissed, then pressed to her heart.

The procession continued down Fleet Street to the fourth tableau, the Israelite judge, Deborah, presiding over nobles, clergy, and commons, with a banner announcing, 'Deborah, consulting for the good government of Israel'.

The final flourish was at Temple Bar, where two giants supported a scroll of verses, summarising the sequence: Elizabeth, born of unity, had acceded to the throne to promote virtue, to govern in consultation with her people, and, guided by the English Bible, to promote the flourishing of the land.

Engraving of Elizabeth I, Queen of England, 1533–1603.

THE TOWER OF LONDON

The Tower of London was, and still is, a mighty fortress with great political and historic significance. Elizabeth followed the tradition of all previous Tudor monarchs, and most medieval ones, in staying there prior to her coronation. It is unlikely to have been an unalloyed pleasure for her, given the Tower's grim connection with her mother, Anne Boleyn, and Elizabeth's own experience as a prisoner there during the reign of her half-sister, Mary I.

The Tower of London is a complex of buildings, at the heart of which is the Norman White Tower, built by William the Conqueror nearly 1000 years ago. It is where monarchs kept their military arsenal, their treasures and their wealth, and it is the place to which they retreated for safety in times of danger. It was also a residence, with royal apartments for the king and queen.

By early 1533, the medieval royal lodgings were in need of repair and modernisation. An extensive programme of works, overseen by Thomas Cromwell, included building a new wing for the new queen, Anne Boleyn, in time for her coronation on 1 June 1533. The old queen's watching chamber was refurbished and retained, whilst a large new suite consisting of presence chamber, long gallery, privy and dining chambers, a bedchamber and three more rooms, was added. All rooms were sumptuously decorated with expensive furnishings and wall hangings.

Shockingly, only three short years later, in May 1536, Anne was back in these same apartments as a prisoner, awaiting her trial and then her execution. In an ironic twist of fate, Anne's daughter, Elizabeth, was also held a prisoner in these apartments some 18 years later. Suspected of involvement in Wyatt's 1554 Rebellion, Elizabeth was arrested and brought to the Tower for interrogation. However, after two months of questioning, no evidence was found against her and she was released to house arrest in the Palace of Woodstock in Oxfordshire. Unsurprisingly, once she was queen, Elizabeth rarely spent any time at the Tower.

By the middle of the Tudor period the Tower's role as a prison for traitors and those considered dangerous to the state had also grown substantially. Henry VIII was the last monarch to use the Tower as a residence. The royal apartments were neglected and fell into disrepair in the 17th century. All that remains of them now are the stone foundations, visible in parts still, on the lawn between the White Tower and the Ravens café.

'Above all earthly treasures, I esteem my people's love'
Elizabeth I

January

1   **Feast of the Circumcision**

Elizabeth presented her own translation of *Mirror of a Sinful Soul* to Katherine Parr (1544)

2   Elizabeth wrote to Edward VI, explaining her long absence from court as due to sickness (1552)

3   Elizabeth approved Richard Fletcher's promotion from Bishop of Worcester to Bishop of London (1595)

4 Roger Ascham, Elizabeth's
tutor, was buried (1569)

5 Catherine de' Medici,
regent to three French
kings, died (1589)

6 Jean de Simier arrived
from France to negotiate a
marriage between François,
Duke of Anjou and
Elizabeth (1579)

JANUARY

7 Troops of Duke of Anjou,
Elizabeth's suitor, defeated
in attempt to take Antwerp
(1583)

8 Elizabeth's ships left
Portsmouth to attack
Newhaven, in France (1563)

9 Michael Moody confessed
to conspiring to make an
assassination attempt on
Elizabeth (1587)

10 Elizabeth's government ordered arrest of all Jesuits (1581)

11 Elizabeth issued a licence to Southampton to hold three fairs a year (1599)

12 Elizabeth travelled by barge from Whitehall to Tower of London to prepare for her coronation (1559)

JANUARY

13 Edmund Spenser, author of
The Faerie Queene, dedicated
to Elizabeth, died (1599)

_____

_____

_____

_____

_____

_____

_____

_____

14 Elizabeth processed from
Tower of London to
Westminster on eve of her
coronation (1559)

_____

_____

_____

_____

_____

_____

_____

15 Elizabeth was crowned
Queen of England (1559)

_____

_____

_____

_____

_____

_____

_____

16 Parliament called for
execution of Mary, Queen
of Scots (1581)

17 Elizabeth was hosted by
Lord Howard de Malden
at Charterhouse, London
(1603)

18 Henry VII of England
married Elizabeth of York
(1486)

JANUARY

19 Elizabeth began a three-day visit to Earl of Nottingham at Chelsea, Middlesex (1600)

20 Elizabeth wrote to Ottoman Sultan, Mahumet (1601)

21 Bill of Attainder passed against Katheryn Howard, Henry VIII's fifth wife (1542)

22 Elizabeth granted musicians Thomas Tallis and William Byrd a 25-year monopoly to print music (1575)

23 Elizabeth officially opened the Royal Exchange in London, founded in 1565 by Sir Thomas Gresham (1571)

24 Thomas Boleyn, Earl of Wiltshire and of Ormond, appointed Lord Privy Seal (1530)

JANUARY

25 **Feast of the Conversion of St Paul**

Elizabeth's first Parliament opened (1559)

26 Thomas Howard, 4th Duke of Norfolk, degraded from Order of the Garter (1572)

27 Francis Drake, courtier and explorer, died in the harbour at Porto Bello (1596)

28 Henry VII of England was born (1457)

Henry VIII of England died (1547)

29 Edward VI and Elizabeth were told of Henry VIII's death (1547)

30 Elizabeth began a three-day visit to The Strand in London, hosted by Sir Robert Cecil (1593)

January

31   Commission convened to
investigate relationship
between Earl of Hertford
and queen's cousin, Lady
Katherine Grey (1562)

Notes

Notes

MONTH PLANNER

February

1 Elizabeth signed death warrant of Mary, Queen of Scots (1587)

2 House of Commons requested Elizabeth to marry (1559)

3 Privy Council issued death warrant of Mary, Queen of Scots (1587)

4 Death warrant of Mary, Queen of Scots was sent to Fotheringhay (1587)

5 Elizabeth stayed in Canterbury, Kent, as a guest of Sir Roger Manwood (1582)

6 The 3,000-strong rebel army of Sir Thomas Wyatt marched on London (1554)

7 Sir Walter Raleigh was imprisoned for brawling (1580)

8 Mary, Queen of Scots was executed at Fotheringhay Castle (1587)

9 Anne Russell, Countess of Warwick, Gentlewoman of the Privy Chamber, died (1604)

10 Elizabeth replied to House of Commons' request for her to marry (1559)

11 Elizabeth taken from Ashridge to Tower of London (1554)

12 Blanche Parry, Chief Gentlewoman of the Privy Chamber, died (1590)

13 Katheryn Howard, Henry VIII's fifth wife, was executed (1542)

14 Elizabeth stayed at Baynard's Castle, the guest of the Earl of Pembroke (1566)

15 Bill for order of church service introduced to House of Commons (1559)

16 Henry VIII was interred at St George's Chapel, Windsor (1547)

17 Sir Thomas Seymour was arrested (1549)

18 Mary I was born (1516)

19 Robert Devereux, Earl of Essex, was tried for treason (1601)

20 Edward VI was crowned King of England & Ireland (1547)

21 Lady Katherine Grey, Elizabeth's cousin, was buried (1568)

22 A sick Elizabeth reached Whitehall, following an eight-day journey from Ashridge (1554)

23 Henry Grey, Duke of Suffolk, father of Lady Jane Grey, executed for his part in Wyatt's Rebellion (1554)

24 Katherine Carey, Countess of Nottingham, Elizabeth's close friend, died (1603)

25 Pope Pius V issued *Regnans in Excelsis*, a bull of excommunication, against Elizabeth (1570)

26 John Dee recommended adoption of a modified Gregorian Calendar (1583)

27 Elizabeth delivered speech to clergy at Somerset Place (1585)

28 Martin Bucer, Protestant reformer, died (1551)

29 John Whitgift, Archbishop of Canterbury, died (1604)

Much suspected by me,
Nothing proved can be,
Quoth Elizabeth
prisoner.

Birthdays	Anniversaries	Reminders	Projects

Gardening	Events	Occasions	Festivals

WYATT'S REBELLION

In 1553, Elizabeth's older half-sister, Mary, became queen. Mary had two aims: to restore England to religious obedience to Rome, and to marry and produce an heir. She was aware that Elizabeth's sympathies were Protestant and did not want the crown to pass to her. Mary's choice of husband was Philip of Spain, heir to vast territories in Europe and the New World.

Dislike of Mary's matrimonial decision was widespread, and a Protestant gentleman, Sir Thomas Wyatt, plotted rebellion. Elizabeth received a letter from the queen requesting her to come to London to avoid any unrest in the countryside. Elizabeth responded that she was too ill to travel. This aroused royal suspicions, as although Wyatt claimed that his aim was just to prevent the match with Philip, most people believed he wanted Elizabeth to take the throne. The government was able to take preventative action to scotch part of the planned uprising, but Wyatt went ahead and marched on London from Kent with a sizeable army. He was defeated in short order, but attention turned to Elizabeth. Whilst she had given no tangible indication of support for the rebels, neither had she made much show of loyalty to Mary. There was evidence that potentially incriminated her – letters sent that she denied receiving

and arrangements made for her to go to a house that, on being questioned, she denied remembering she even owned. A copy of one of her letters was also found in the possession of the French ambassador. On 12th February, still ill, Elizabeth was obliged to travel to Whitehall. For three weeks she was unable to enter her half-sister's presence as investigations continued. When Wyatt admitted that she had sent him a reply to a message recommending her to stay away from London, it was considered sufficient to send her to the Tower, and the Marquis of Winchester and the Earl of Sussex were deputed to take her. Frantic, Elizabeth begged for time to write to her half-sister. The letter protested her innocence vehemently and appealed to Mary not to let her be convicted unheard. No substantive evidence emerged against Elizabeth, and the queen, although suspicious, was adamant that her half-sister could not be convicted without solid proof. After Wyatt's execution in April, Elizabeth's confinement in the Tower became less onerous and she was released to house arrest at Woodstock in Oxfordshire, under the supervision of Sir Henry Bedingfield.

Theobalds

Theobolds (pronounced 'Tibbalds') was a country house built by Sir William Cecil, Lord Burghley, Elizabeth's Chief Minister and a leading patron of architecture in Elizabethan England. It became the largest and most extravagant of the magnificent prodigy houses built during the period.

Located near Cheshunt in Hertfordshire, its proximity to London (it was only some 14 miles from Westminster) and the adjacent large, well-stocked hunting park added to its appeal. Elizabeth was a regular visitor, and, over time, Cecil developed and expanded the property to meet her requirements, as well as his own.

When Cecil bought Theobalds in 1564, it was an unprepossessing moated manor house which he initially replaced with a modest courtyard house. However, from the late 1560s he began an ambitious building programme that re-built the house on a vast scale, turning it into the largest private house in England. When completed, it had five courtyards, extending across a quarter-mile axis, all the rooms and facilities Cecil needed to meet his own obligations and to fulfil the business of state, plus sufficient lodgings for the aristocrats and their servants who accompanied Elizabeth on her visits.

Unusually, in addition to these lodgings, Theobalds also contained separate suites of rooms dedicated to the queen's use. Kenilworth and Burghley House, another of Cecil's houses, were the only other private houses in the country to have rooms reserved for the monarch.

Elizabeth made more than a dozen visits to Theobalds, some brief and some of much longer duration. One visit, beginning on 24 February 1573, lasted two weeks. During these visits Elizabeth received and entertained ambassadors and other foreign dignitaries, displaying the full splendour of Theobalds to the international gaze.

Theobald's glorious buildings were accompanied by spectacular gardens, divided into the Privy Garden and the Great Garden. The latter covered more than seven acres and a description from 1598 refers to its nine knot gardens, 70 feet square, each with a white marble fountain in the middle and a canal that enabled visitors to pass through the garden by boat.

Elizabeth's successor, King James VI & I, was also greatly enamoured of Theobalds. In 1607, in an exchange with Sir William's son, Robert, he gave up the Old Palace at Hatfield for ownership of Theobalds. Sadly, this fabulous house was demolished after the Civil War and all that remains today are some fragments of building and garden wall.

FEBRUARY

1 Elizabeth signed death
warrant of Mary, Queen of
Scots (1587)

2 **Feast of the Purification of
the Virgin (Candlemas)**

House of Commons
requested Elizabeth to
marry (1559)

3 Privy Council issued death
warrant of Mary, Queen of
Scots (1587)

4   Death warrant of Mary,
Queen of Scots was sent to
Fotheringhay (1587)

5   Elizabeth stayed in
Canterbury, Kent, as
a guest of Sir Roger
Manwood (1582)

6   The 3,000-strong rebel
army of Sir Thomas Wyatt
marched on London (1554)

FEBRUARY

7 Sir Walter Raleigh was
imprisoned for brawling
(1580)

8 Mary, Queen of Scots was
executed at Fotheringhay
Castle (1587)

9 Anne Russell, Countess of
Warwick, Gentlewoman
of the Privy Chamber, died
(1604)

10 Elizabeth replied to House
of Commons' request for
her to marry (1559)

11 Elizabeth taken from
Ashridge to Tower of
London (1554)

12 Blanche Parry, Chief
Gentlewoman of the Privy
Chamber, died (1590)

FEBRUARY

13 Katheryn Howard, Henry
VIII's fifth wife, was
executed (1542)

14 Elizabeth stayed at
Baynard's Castle, guest of
the Earl of Pembroke (1566)

15 Bill for order of church
service introduced to House
of Commons (1559)

16 Henry VIII was interred
at St George's Chapel,
Windsor (1547)

_____

_____

_____

_____

_____

_____

_____

17 Sir Thomas Seymour was
arrested (1549)

_____

_____

_____

_____

_____

_____

_____

18 Mary I was born (1516)

_____

_____

_____

_____

_____

_____

_____

FEBRUARY

19 Robert Devereux, Earl of
Essex, was tried for treason
(1601)

20 Edward VI was crowned
King of England & Ireland
(1547)

21 Lady Katherine Grey,
Elizabeth cousin, was
buried (1568)

22 A sick Elizabeth reached Whitehall, following an eight-day journey from Ashridge (1554)

23 Henry Grey, Duke of Suffolk, father of Lady Jane Grey, executed for his part in Wyatt's Rebellion (1554)

24 **St Matthias' Day**

Katherine Carey, Countess of Nottingham, Elizabeth's close friend, died (1603)

FEBRUARY

25 Pope Pius V issued *Regnans in Excelsis*, a bull of excommunication, against Elizabeth (1570)

26 John Dee recommended adoption of a modified Gregorian Calendar (1583)

27 St Leander's Day

Elizabeth delivered speech to clergy at Somerset Place (1585)

28 Martin Bucer, Protestant
reformer, died (1551)

_____

_____

_____

_____

_____

_____

_____

_____

29 John Whitgift, Archbishop
of Canterbury, died (1604)

_____

_____

_____

_____

_____

_____

_____

Notes

_____

_____

_____

_____

_____

_____

_____

February

Notes

Notes

MONTH PLANNER

March

1   Elizabeth expelled Dutch Protestant refugees operating as privateers from England (1572)

2   After banishing Lettice Knollys for marrying Leicester in 1578, Elizabeth granted her an audience (1598)

3   Shakespeare's *Henry VI* was performed at the Rose Theatre (1592)

4   Henry Carey, Lord Hunsdon, Elizabeth's maternal cousin, was born (1526)

5   Bill of Attainder passed against Sir Thomas Seymour for plotting to kidnap Edward VI and marry Elizabeth (1549)

6   Elizabeth was hosted by Robert Dudley, Earl of Leicester, at Gray's Inn, London (1565)

7   Elizabeth wrote to Lord Protector Somerset requesting release of her servants from the Tower (1549)

8   Elizabeth stayed at Gorhambury, Hertfordshire, as a guest of Sir Nicholas Bacon (1573)

9   Lady Margaret Douglas, Countess of Lennox died (1578)

10   William Paulet, 1st Marquis of Winchester, Lord High Treasurer, died (1572)

11   Elizabeth stayed at Somerset Place (1583)

12   Sir Thomas Boleyn, Earl of Wiltshire and Ormond died (1539)

13   John Woolton, Bishop of Exeter, died from an asthma attack (1594)

14   Henri IV of France led Anglo-French troops to victory over the Catholic League (1590)

15   Elizabeth made a closing speech to Parliament (1576)

16   Elizabeth granted audience to new Spanish ambassador, Bernardino de Mendoza (1578)

17   Held at Whitehall on Mary I's orders, Elizabeth wrote to her, pleading for an audience (1554)

18   Elizabeth was sent to Tower of London, suspected of involvement in Wyatt's Rebellion (1554)

19   Mme de Chatillon entertained Elizabeth at Ham House, Surrey (1570)

20   Sir Thomas Seymour, Baron Sudeley, was executed (1549)

21   Cardinal de Chatillon died at Canterbury (1571)

22   The 1559 Act of Supremacy finished its passage through Parliament (1559)

23   Privy Council advised Elizabeth that Mary, Queen of Scots and François II of France were her mortal enemies (1560)

24   Elizabeth died at Richmond Palace (1603)

25   Sir Walter Raleigh granted patent to found colony of Virginia (1584)

26   Robert Carey announced Elizabeth's death to James VI (1603)

27   Robert Devereux, 2nd Earl of Essex departed to take up post of Lord Lieutenant of Ireland (1599)

28   William Cecil, 2nd Earl of Salisbury, was born (1591)

29   Elizabeth made her closing speech to Parliament (1585)

30   Mary, Queen of Scots responded to Elizabeth's suggestion that she marry Lord Robert Dudley (1564)

31   Public debate held between Catholics and Protestants (1559)

Birthdays	Anniversaries	Reminders	Projects

Gardening	Events	Occasions	Festivals

THE SEYMOUR SCANDAL

On 28th January 1547, aged 13, Elizabeth was orphaned when her father, Henry VIII, died. She went to live in the household of her stepmother, the dowager-queen Katherine Parr, with whom she had a warm and affectionate relationship. Soon, however, there was a new member of the household. Before May was out, Katherine had secretly married. Her husband was Sir Thomas Seymour, brother of Henry VIII's third wife, and thus uncle of the new king, Elizabeth's half-brother, Edward VI. Katherine and Seymour had been courting before the king's eye had fallen on her, so it was a marriage of affection on her part, at least, and probably on his, although he had been putting out feelers for a marriage with either Elizabeth or her half-sister, Mary, before the wedding to Katherine.

The marriage caused controversy amongst the king's councillors, but Katherine, Seymour and Elizabeth were happy, whiling away the spring days at Katherine's house at Chelsea. Soon, events took a darker turn. Seymour began indulging in what was at best horse-play, and at worst sexual advances towards Elizabeth. He would go into her bedroom early, still in his night-clothes, and tickle and tease her whilst she burrowed, laughing and shrieking, deeper into the bed. Her governess,

Katherine Astley, remonstrated with him, but he laughed it off. Mrs Astley raised the matter with Katherine, who sought to defuse the situation by joining the games. On one occasion, Katherine held Elizabeth's arms whilst Seymour slashed her gown with his dagger. But Seymour went too far, and Katherine, by now pregnant, found the two locked in an embrace. Appalled, she gave Elizabeth a kind, but firm, lecture on the necessity of preserving her reputation and sent her away. Elizabeth understood Katherine had only her best interests at heart, and thanked her for her care, but she would never see her beloved stepmother again. Katherine died of childbed fever in September 1548. Seymour, who had been envious of his brother's power as Lord Protector, began plotting against him, and wrote to Elizabeth's household officers, suggesting they should influence her to marry him. Before long, his reckless behaviour resulted in his execution for treason. Elizabeth was closely questioned, amidst rumours that she was pregnant by him. She indignantly rebutted every accusation, and for the remainder of her brother's reign was careful to act as the most virtuous, demure, and studious young woman in the kingdom.

Richmond Palace

Located by the river in what is now known as Richmond-upon-Thames, Richmond Palace was one of Elizabeth's favourite residences, second only to Greenwich, and it is the palace in which she died.

The medieval kings built a variety of residences at what was then the royal manor of Sheen and in the fourteenth century Edward III developed the existing royal manor house into a riverside palace. In the fifteenth century Henry V re-built the Palace of Sheen as a collection of principally timber-framed buildings adjacent to a moat within which sat a massive three-storey stone tower. On 22nd December 1497, when Henry VII and his court were staying at Sheen, fire broke out in the king's lodgings and most of the palace, and the wooden areas in particular, were severely damaged or destroyed.

Henry VII re-built the palace complex in brick, retaining the three-storey stone tower into which he put his privy lodgings. To the east of the lodgings were an orchard, extensive gardens, and a recreation area with a bowling alley, tennis courts and archery butts, surrounded by a new style of timber-framed two-storey galleries. Works were completed in 1501, in time to host a magnificent wedding feast for

Prince Arthur and Katharine of Aragon. Henry VII renamed the restored palace Richmond, and it became his favourite residence. It was also where he died in April 1509.

Henry VIII used Richmond Palace in the early days of his reign but rarely after 1530, once he had Whitehall and Hampton Court Palace. He gave it to his fourth wife, Anne of Cleves, as part of her annulment settlement and she used it regularly between 1540 and 1548, when it was taken back by Edward VI.

Elizabeth shared her grandfather's love of Richmond Palace, visiting it frequently. When there, she used the king's privy apartments (rather than the queen's), as at Whitehall. It is to Richmond that Elizabeth brought the Duke of Anjou in 1579 when he was travelling incognito to woo Elizabeth in person, and they spent most of his ten-day visit here. During their stay they enjoyed riding in Richmond Park. Situated close to the palace, it was a royal hunting ground in the Tudor period and remains a Royal Park today.

Richmond Palace was sold during the Commonwealth and all that remains today is the main gateway and part of the outer range that faces onto Richmond Green.

MARCH

1   Elizabeth expelled Dutch
Protestant refugees
operating as privateers from
England (1572)

2   After banishing Lettice
Knollys for marrying
Leicester in 1578, Elizabeth
granted her an audience
(1598)

3   Shakespeare's *Henry VI*
was performed at the Rose
Theatre (1592)

4   Henry Carey, Lord
Hunsdon, Elizabeth's
maternal cousin, was born
(1526)

_____

_____

_____

_____

_____

_____

_____

_____

5   Bill of Attainder was
passed against Sir Thomas
Seymour for plotting to
kidnap Edward VI and
marry Elizabeth (1549)

_____

_____

_____

_____

_____

_____

_____

6   Elizabeth was hosted by
Robert Dudley, Earl of
Leicester, at Gray's Inn,
London (1565)

_____

_____

_____

_____

_____

_____

MARCH

7 Elizabeth wrote to Lord
Protector Somerset
requesting release of her
servants from the Tower
(1549)

8 Elizabeth stayed at
Gorhambury, Hertfordshire,
as a guest of Sir Nicholas
Bacon (1573)

9 Lady Margaret Douglas,
Countess of Lennox died
(1578)

10 William Paulet, 1st
Marquis of Winchester,
Lord High Treasurer, died
(1572)

11 Elizabeth stayed at
Somerset Place (1583)

12 Sir Thomas Boleyn, Earl
of Wiltshire and Ormond
died (1539)

13 John Woolton, Bishop of
Exeter, died from an asthma
attack (1594)

_____

_____

_____

_____

_____

_____

_____

14 Henri IV of France led
Anglo-French troops to
victory over the Catholic
League (1590)

_____

_____

_____

_____

_____

_____

_____

15 Elizabeth made her closing
speech to Parliament (1576)

_____

_____

_____

_____

_____

_____

_____

16 Elizabeth granted an
audience to the new
Spanish ambassador,
Bernardino de Mendoza
(1578)

17 Held at Whitehall on
Mary I's orders, Elizabeth
wrote to her pleading for an
audience (1554)

18 Elizabeth was sent
to Tower of London,
suspected of involvement in
Wyatt's Rebellion (1554)

MARCH

19 Mme de Chatillon
entertained Elizabeth at
Ham House, Surrey (1570)

_____

_____

_____

_____

_____

_____

_____

_____

20 Sir Thomas Seymour,
Baron Sudeley, was executed
(1549)

_____

_____

_____

_____

_____

_____

_____

21 Cardinal de Chatillon died
at Canterbury (1571)

_____

_____

_____

_____

_____

_____

_____

22 The 1559 Act of Supremacy finished its passage through Parliament (1559)

Easter Sunday – 1573, 1598

23 Privy Council advised Elizabeth that Mary, Queen of Scots and François II of France were her mortal enemies (1560)

24 Elizabeth died at Richmond Palace (1603)

25 **The Annunciation of the Virgin Mary**

Sir Walter Raleigh granted patent to found colony of Virginia (1584)

Easter Sunday – 1543, 1554

26 Robert Carey announced Elizabeth's death to James VI at Holyroodhouse, Edinburgh (1603)

Easter Sunday – 1559, 1570, 1581, 1595

27 Robert Devereux, 2nd Earl of Essex departed to take up post of Lord Lieutenant of Ireland (1599)

28 William Cecil, 2nd Earl of
Salisbury, was born (1591)

Easter Sunday – 1535, 1540

29 Elizabeth made her closing
speech to Parliament (1585)

Easter Sunday – 1551,
1562, 1587, 1592

30 Mary, Queen of Scots
responded to Elizabeth's
suggestion that she marry
Lord Robert Dudley (1564)

Easter Sunday – 1567, 1578

MARCH

31 Public debate held between
Catholics and Protestants
(1559)

_____

_____

_____

_____

_____

_____

_____

_____

Notes

_____

_____

_____

_____

_____

_____

_____

_____

_____

_____

_____

_____

_____

_____

_____

_____

_____

_____

_____

_____

MARCH

Notes

MONTH PLANNER

April

1   James VI wrote to his 'dearest sister', Elizabeth, requesting her seal on an agreement (1586)

2   Treaty of Cateau-Cambrésis, ending war with France, was signed (1559)

3   Elizabeth Howard, Countess of Wiltshire, Elizabeth's grandmother, died (1538)

4   Elizabeth knighted Francis Drake on the *Golden Hind* (1581)

5   John Stowe, antiquarian of London, died (1605)

6   Sir Francis Walsingham, Secretary of State and spymaster for Elizabeth, died (1590)

7   Elizabeth announced Peace of Cateau-Cambrésis (1559)

8   Elizabeth urged the Earl of Huntingdon to take care of his health (1594)

9   Sir Walter Raleigh's expedition that resulted in founding of Roanoake Colony, departed England (1585)

10   Elizabeth responded to Parliament's request for her to marry in her closing speech (1563)

11   Sir Thomas Wyatt was executed for his rebellion against Mary I (1554)

12   William Cecil, Lord Burghley, created Knight of the Garter (1572)

13   London's clergy accepted Oath of Succession, naming Elizabeth as heir to the English throne (1534)

14   Earl of Essex took up post of Lord Lieutenant in Dublin (1599)

15   Elizabeth Throckmorton was born (1565)

16   Elizabeth was a guest of Sir Thomas Cecil at Wimbledon, Surrey (1592)

17   Sir Thomas More was taken to Tower of London for refusing Oath of Supremacy (1534)

18   John Leland, antiquarian, died (1552)

19   Francis Drake led pre-emptive strike against Spanish fleet in Cadiz (1587)

20   Lady Mary Grey died (1578)

21   Henry VII died and his son, Henry VIII, ascended the throne (1509)

22   Elizabeth excused a sick Lord Burghley from attendance at annual Garter ceremony (1593)

23   Lord Robert Dudley created Knight of the Garter (1559)

24   Mary, Queen of Scots married François, Dauphin of France, at Notre Dame in Paris (1558)

25   Elizabeth was guest of the Earl of Pembroke at Baynard's Castle, London (1559)

26   Katherine Carey, Elizabeth's maternal cousin, married Sir Francis Knollys (1540)

27   Elizabeth Throckmorton returned to court as a maid-of-honour (1592)

28   Elizabeth's funeral was held at Westminster Abbey (1603)

29   Elizabeth attended wedding of the Marquis of Northampton and Helena Snakenborg (1571)

30   Elizabeth stayed at Wanstead, Essex, as a guest of Robert Dudley (1579)

Birthdays	Anniversaries	Reminders	Projects

Gardening	Events	Occasions	Festivals

ELIZABETH'S FUNERAL

Elizabeth celebrated the Christmas of 1602 with gusto – there was dancing, bear-baiting and gambling for high stakes. The following month, she moved to her favourite palace of Richmond, where she entertained the Venetian ambassador in February, looking as magnificent as ever in her bejewelled gowns and ruffs. Towards the end of that month, however, she became depressed and withdrawn. The immediate cause was the death of her cousin, Katherine Carey, Countess of Nottingham, one of her oldest friends. The queen refused to leave her own rooms, and despite the best efforts of her courtiers, sank into gloom. She rejected medicine, and her appetite, never large, disappeared. She descended into a silent, motionless state, refusing to eat or lie down. By late March she was too weak to stand, and lay in bed, barely speaking, comforted only by the presence of the Archbishop of Canterbury, who knelt beside her in prayer for hours. Elizabeth died early in the morning of 24th March and by ten o'clock her successor, James VI of Scotland, had been proclaimed as James I of England.

As Elizabeth had always feared, her courtiers turned immediately to the rising sun, leaving her body at Richmond whilst they rushed to ingratiate themselves with James.

At last, her remains were wrapped in black velvet and conveyed at night by river to Whitehall, where she lay in state until 28th April. The funeral James ordered was magnificent. The procession to Westminster Abbey was led by 240 poor women. They were followed by all the queen's servants, household officials, ministers and clergymen, from the most menial to the Archbishop of Canterbury. Elizabeth's lead coffin, covered in purple velvet and with a painted effigy of the queen, was carried on a chariot, pulled by four grey horses trapped in black velvet with the arms of England and France. Following the coffin were the Master of Horse, the Lord Admiral, and the wives and daughters of the nobility. Finally, the Yeomen of the Guard, halberds inverted, completed the procession. It was reported that there was 'such a general sighing, groaning and weeping as the like hath not been seen or known in the memory of man'.

James VI & I paid £1,485 for the magnificent monument that covers Elizabeth's tomb. Her marble effigy, sculpted by Maximilian Colt, shows her in full ceremonial garb, with crown and sceptre.

WESTMINSTER ABBEY

Elizabeth was crowned in Westminster Abbey and this iconic monument to 1000 years of English history is her final resting place too.

The ceremonial heart of the English monarchy since the days of Edward the Confessor, Westminster Abbey has also become a symbol of national commemoration to treasured public figures; statesmen, writers, scientists and musicians alike. All English monarchs since William the Conqueror have been crowned in the Abbey, including Henry III, who had his second coronation here. It is the burial place of 17 monarchs, and more than 3,300 other individuals. These include all the Tudor monarchs, with the exception of Henry VIII, who was laid to rest at St George's Chapel, Windsor.

Following her funeral service on 28th April 1603, Elizabeth was interred with her grandparents, Henry VII and Elizabeth of York, in the Lady Chapel. The Lady Chapel, with its spectacular fan-vaulted ceiling, was built by Henry VII to provide a chantry chapel and mausoleum for his dynasty. He and Elizabeth of York have a central position in the east of the chapel, under a magnificent marble tomb with gilt-bronze effigies created by Florentine Renaissance sculptor Pietro Torrigiano. Elizabeth's great-grandmother, Lady Margaret Beaufort, is buried in the Lady Chapel, as are her half-brother, Edward VI, and half-sister, Mary I. Her step-mother, Anne of Cleves, the only one of Henry VIII's wives buried at the Abbey, is close by, near the high altar in the Sacrarium.

In 1606 Elizabeth's body was moved from her grandparents' tomb to a vault under the north aisle of the Lady Chapel, where her coffin was placed on top of that of her half-sister Mary's. An elaborate white marble tomb marks the spot. Oddly, the tomb only has an effigy of Elizabeth, and Mary I is mentioned just once on the tomb's inscription.

In 1612 James VI & I arranged for the remains of his mother, Mary, Queen of Scots, to be brought from Peterborough Cathedral and reinterred in an impressive tomb (larger than that provided for Elizabeth) on the south aisle in the Lady Chapel, close to the tomb of her aunt and mother-in-law, Margaret Douglas, Countess of Lennox.

It is possible to visit Westminster Abbey and to see the coronation chair used by Elizabeth, and, indeed, all monarchs since 1308. The Queen's Diamond Jubilee Galleries display many priceless treasures from the Abbey's collection; Elizabeth's reconstructed funeral effigy, corset from her original funeral effigy, and her 'Essex' ring are among them.

APRIL

1 James VI wrote to his 'dearest sister', Elizabeth, requesting her to seal their agreement (1586)

Easter Sunday – 1537, 1548, 1584

2 Treaty of Cateau-Cambrésis, ending war with France, was signed (1559)

Easter Sunday – 1553, 1564, 1589, 1600

3 Elizabeth Howard, Countess of Wiltshire, Elizabeth's grandmother, died (1538)

Easter Sunday – 1575, 1580

4   Elizabeth knighted Francis
Drake on the *Golden Hind*
(1581)

5   John Stowe, antiquarian of
London, died (1605)

Easter Sunday – 1534,
1545, 1556

6   Sir Francis Walsingham,
Secretary of State and
spymaster for Elizabeth,
died (1590)

Easter Sunday – 1539,
1550, 1561, 1572, 1586,
1597

APRIL

7   Elizabeth announced Peace
of Cateau-Cambrésis (1559)

Easter Sunday – 1577, 1602

8   Elizabeth urged Earl of
Huntingdon to take care of
his health (1594)

9   Sir Walter Raleigh's
expedition that resulted
in founding of Roanoake
Colony, departed England
(1585)

Easter Sunday – 1542

10 Elizabeth responded to
Parliament's request for
her to marry in her closing
speech (1563)

Easter Sunday – 1547,
1558, 1569, 1583, 1594

11 Sir Thomas Wyatt was
executed for his rebellion
against Mary I (1554)

Easter Sunday – 1563,
1574, 1599

12 William Cecil, Lord
Burghley, created Knight of
the Garter (1572)

APRIL

13 London's clergy accepted
Oath of Succession, naming
Elizabeth as heir to the
English throne (1534)

Easter Sunday – 1544

14 Earl of Essex took up post
of Lord Lieutenant in
Dublin (1599)

Easter Sunday – 1555, 1560,
1566, 1591, 1596

15 Elizabeth Throckmorton
was born (1565)

Easter Sunday – 1571, 1582

16 Elizabeth was a guest
of Sir Thomas Cecil at
Wimbledon, Surrey (1592)

Easter Sunday – 1536

17 Sir Thomas More was
taken to Tower of London
for refusing to accept Oath
of Supremacy (1534)

Easter Sunday – 1541,
1552, 1588

18 John Leland, antiquarian,
died (1552)

Easter Sunday – 1557,
1568, 1593

APRIL

19 Francis Drake led
pre-emptive strike against
Spanish fleet in Cadiz
(1587)

Easter Sunday – 1579

20 Lady Mary Grey died
(1578)

21 Henry VII, died and his
son, Henry VIII, ascended
the throne (1509)

Easter Sunday – 1538, 1549,
1585

22 Elizabeth excused a sick
Lord Burghley from
attendance at the annual
Garter ceremony (1593)

Easter Sunday – 1565,
1576, 1590, 1601

23 Lord Robert Dudley
created Knight of the
Garter (1559)

24 Mary, Queen of Scots
married François, Dauphin
of France, at Notre Dame
in Paris (1558)

APRIL

25 **St Mark's Day**

Elizabeth was the guest
of Earl of Pembroke at
Baynard's Castle, London
(1559)

Easter Sunday – 1546

26 Katherine Carey,
Elizabeth's maternal cousin,
married Sir Francis Knollys
(1540)

27 Elizabeth Throckmorton
returned to court as a
maid-of-honour (1592)

28 Elizabeth's funeral was
held at Westminster Abbey
(1603)

29 Elizabeth attended
wedding of the Marquis of
Northampton and Helena
Snakenborg (1571)

30 Elizabeth stayed at
Wanstead, Essex, as a guest
of Robert Dudley (1579)

APRIL

Notes

Notes

MONTH PLANNER

May

1 Elizabeth refused to receive a Papal Nuncio or to send delegates to the Council of Trent (1561)

2 Anne Boleyn arrested for treason and taken to the Tower of London (1536)

3 Sir Edward Rogers, courtier and MP, died (1568)

4 Walter Devereux and Edward Fiennes de Clinton created earls of Essex and Lincoln, respectively (1572)

5 Sir Henry Sidney, formerly Lord Deputy of Ireland, died (1586)

6 Elizabeth was the guest of the Earl and Countess of Pembroke at Baynard's Castle, London (1575)

7 James VI of Scotland arrived in London to claim the English throne (1603)

8 Elizabeth ratified the Act of Uniformity (1559)

9 Margaret Douglas, Countess of Lennox, was arrested for suspected treason (1562)

10 Elizabeth stayed at Leicester House, London, with Robert Dudley, Earl of Leicester (1577)

11 Thomas Kyd, playwright, was sought in hunt for source of anti-foreigner tracts (1593)

12 William Brereton and others were found guilty of adultery with Anne Boleyn (1536)

13 Mary, Queen of Scots was defeated at the Battle of Langside (1568)

14 Elizabeth wrote to the Duke of Anjou regarding his intervention in the war in the Netherlands (1572)

15 Elizabeth sent her portrait to Edward VI (1549)

16 Mary, Queen of Scots arrived in England after crossing the Solway Firth in a fishing-boat (1568)

17 Matthew Parker, Archbishop of Canterbury, died (1575)

18 Thomas Wyatt was hanged, drawn and quartered after leading a rebellion (1554)

19 Anne Boleyn was executed (1536)

20 Elizabeth was reconciled with Mary I at Hampton Court (1555)

21 Sir Martin Frobisher, explorer and privateer, attended Elizabeth's court (1578)

22 Edward Seymour, later Earl of Hertford, was born (1539)

23 Elizabeth was brought to Woodstock Palace under house arrest (1554)

24 Copy of *Regnans in Excelsis*, excommunicating Elizabeth, nailed to Bishop of London's palace door (1570)

25 Elizabeth signed two-year passport for Sir Philip Sidney (1572)

26 First French hostages under the Treaty of Cateau-Cambrésis arrived at the English court (1559)

27 Elizabeth stayed at Nonsuch Palace in Surrey (1580)

28 Edinburgh Castle fell to the supporters of James VI, ending the Lang Siege (1573)

29 Mary, Queen of Scots and her husband, François, ratified the Treaty of Norham (1559)

30 Sir Francis Knollys and Lord Scrope reported to Elizabeth on their meeting with Mary, Queen of Scots (1568)

31 Elizabeth wrote to Privy Council regarding land dispute with Earl of Bedford (1553)

Birthdays	Anniversaries	Reminders	Projects

Gardening	Events	Occasions	Festivals

THE RELIGIOUS SETTLEMENT

On 8th May 1559, Elizabeth gave Royal Assent to the Act of Supremacy recognising her as Supreme Governor of the Church in England. Religion had been the first matter which Elizabeth had wished to settle on her accession. As matters stood on the death of Mary I, England was a Catholic nation, within the obedience of Rome. Most of the queen's subjects were Catholic in doctrine, but, excepting the bishops, few were committed to papal obedience. The death of the Catholic Archbishop Pole and the nomination of Elizabeth's choice, Parker, to replace him, together with vacancies in 10 of the 26 bishoprics, limited the clergy's ability to combine against the queen's largely Protestant council.

When Parliament opened in January, the first item of business brought forward by the Lord Keeper, as Elizabeth's representative, was the necessity to make an order for uniformity in religion. This was a clear indication that Elizabeth would not be content with England remaining in the Catholic fold. The House of Commons was favourable to Protestantism, but the Lords, which included a largely Catholic nobility, as well as the bishops, was not. The Commons sent a bill to the Lords which abolished papal supremacy, vesting it in the Crown, and reinstated the Protestant Prayer Book of 1552, along with harsh penalties for non-conformity. The Lords mauled the bill, ending only with a proposition that Elizabeth might take the title of Head of the Church, but not reinstituting the Protestant service. This bill was modified further to meet the objection that a woman could not be Supreme Head of the Church by naming Elizabeth as 'Governor'. Denying her this title would result, after a third offence, in a conviction for treason.

Simultaneously, an Act of Uniformity was introduced, again putting forward the 1552 Prayer Book, although with modifications which would allow Catholics to conform to the law without excessive violation of their consciences. Many of the ceremonies and ornaments of the old faith were retained, including clerical vestments. Much to Elizabeth's personal distaste, clergy were permitted to marry. The bill passed the Commons. It might still have been rejected by the Lords, but an excuse had been found to keep two of the bishops in the Tower and the bill passed by a majority of three. This religious settlement, which the radicals hoped was just a staging post, was defended by Elizabeth to her dying day.

WOODSTOCK

Elizabeth was held under house arrest at the royal manor at Woodstock from May 1554 to April 1555 on the orders of her half-sister, Mary I.

Located in Oxfordshire, the royal manor with its large hunting parks was popular with the medieval kings, and it was also liked and used frequently by the first two Tudor kings. Henry VII spent significant sums of money improving it and Henry VIII was a regular visitor, with some lengthy stays. He spent Easter 1518 at Woodstock, to avoid the plague, and in autumn 1523 the Court resided there for several months. Only six of the king's houses, known as the 'greater houses', were large enough to accommodate the whole court and Woodstock was the only one outside the Thames Valley.

It comprised two courtyards, with the royal lodgings in the inner courtyard. These were unusual in that the king's and the queen's lodgings each had a great hall and privy chambers. The king's great hall was especially large and approached by a notable flight of 35 stairs. The queen's bedroom was linked to the king's drawing room by a privy chamber, providing private access for the couple.

Elizabeth was held in the queen's lodgings, which, although spacious and impressive, were cold, draughty and in need of repair. The medieval house, with its various rooms, staircases and numerous windows, was not suited to be a secure prison, so additional guards were posted in and around the manor. Despite this experience, once queen, Elizabeth visited some five or six times on her summer progresses. She spent more than a month there in 1575, during which extensive entertainment, including masques and dramatic performances, were staged in the manor's private garden. Elizabeth actively participated in the spectacles staged for her, hosted and overseen by Sir Henry Lee, Steward and Lieutenant of Woodstock. The account of this entertainment is the earliest surviving text of Elizabeth's reception in a private garden.

Today, nothing remains of Woodstock Palace. It was severely damaged during the Civil War and subsequently looted for building materials by the local people. In 1704 Queen Anne gave Woodstock estate to the Duke of Marlborough following his victory at the Battle of Blenheim. He built the glorious Blenheim Palace and the remains of Woodstock were removed as part of the substantial associated landscaping. A small monument in the grounds now marks the site of Woodstock manor.

MAY

1   **SS Philip and James the Less, the Apostles' Day**

Elizabeth refused to receive a Papal Nuncio or to send delegates to the Council of Trent (1561)

2   Anne Boleyn was arrested for treason and taken to the Tower of London (1536)

3   Sir Edward Rogers, courtier and MP, died (1568)

4 Walter Devereux and
Edward Fiennes de Clinton
created earls of Essex and
Lincoln, respectively (1572)

5 Sir Henry Sidney, formerly
Lord Deputy of Ireland,
died (1586)

6 Elizabeth was the guest
of the Earl and Countess
of Pembroke at Baynard's
Castle, London (1575)

MAY

7 James VI of Scotland
arrived in London to claim
the English throne (1603)

8 Elizabeth ratified the Act of
Uniformity (1559)

9 Margaret Douglas,
Countess of Lennox, was
arrested for suspected
treason (1562)

10   Elizabeth stayed at
Leicester House, London,
with Robert Dudley, Earl
of Leicester (1577)

11   Thomas Kyd, playwright,
was sought in hunt for
source of anti-foreigner
tracts (1593)

12   William Brereton and
others were found guilty of
adultery with Anne Boleyn
(1536)

MAY

13   Mary, Queen of Scots was
defeated at the Battle of
Langside (1568)

14   Elizabeth wrote to the
Duke of Anjou regarding
his intervention in the war
in the Netherlands (1572)

15   Elizabeth sent her portrait
to Edward VI (1549)

16 Mary, Queen of Scots
arrived in England after
crossing the Solway Firth
in a fishing-boat (1568)

17 Matthew Parker,
Archbishop of Canterbury,
died (1575)

18 Thomas Wyatt was hanged,
drawn and quartered after
leading a rebellion (1554)

MAY

19 Anne Boleyn was executed (1536)

20 Elizabeth was reconciled with Mary I at Hampton Court (1555)

21 Sir Martin Frobisher, explorer and privateer, attended Elizabeth's court (1578)

22 Edward Seymour, later
Earl of Hertford, was born
(1539)

23 Elizabeth was brought to
Woodstock Palace under
house arrest (1554)

24 Copy of *Regnans in
Excelsis*, excommunicating
Elizabeth, nailed to Bishop
of London's palace door
(1570)

MAY

25 Elizabeth signed two-year passport for Sir Philip Sidney (1572)

26 First French hostages, under the Treaty of Cateau-Cambrésis arrived at the English court (1559)

27 Elizabeth stayed at Nonsuch Palace in Surrey (1580)

28 Edinburgh Castle fell to the supporters of James VI, ending the Lang Siege (1573)

29 Mary, Queen of Scots and her husband, François, ratified the Treaty of Norham (1559)

30 Sir Francis Knollys and Lord Scrope reported to Elizabeth on their meeting with Mary, Queen of Scots (1568)

MAY

31 Elizabeth wrote to Privy
Council regarding land
dispute with Earl of Bedford
(1553)

Notes

Notes

Month planner

June

1 Anne Boleyn, pregnant with Elizabeth, was crowned Queen of England (1533)
2 Thomas Howard, 4th Duke of Norfolk, was executed for treason (1572)
3 Earl of Essex's expedition left England for Cadiz, Spain (1596)
4 Elizabeth wrote to Earl and Countess of Shrewsbury, joking about the Earl of Leicester's new eating regime (1577)
5 Anne Cecil, Countess of Oxford, daughter of Sir William Cecil, died (1588)
6 Robert Cecil, son of Sir William Cecil, was baptised (1563)
7 Roderigo Lopez was executed for allegedly trying to poison Elizabeth (1594)
8 Elizabeth stayed with Sir Thomas Gresham at Osterley, Middlesex (1571)
9 Thomas Radcliffe, 3rd Earl of Sussex, died (1583)
10 François, Duke of Anjou, Elizabeth's last serious suitor, died (1584)
11 Marie of Guise, Queen and Regent of Scotland, died (1560)
12 Lord Deputy and Council of Ireland excused themselves to Elizabeth after granting Edward Fitton a pardon for murder (1573)
13 Final night of Elizabeth's eight-day stay at Hatfield Palace (1575)
14 Thomas Wharton, 2nd Baron Wharton, died (1572)
15 Elizabeth Knollys was born (1549)
16 Lady Russell and Lord Cobham entertained Elizabeth at Blackfriars (1600)
17 Edward VI altered his 'Devise for the Succession' to leave the throne to Lady Jane Grey (1553)

18 Robert Devereux, 2nd Earl of Essex, succeeded his stepfather, Leicester, as Master of the Horse (1587)
19 James VI & I, Elizabeth's successor, was born (1566)
20 Countess of Lennox sent to Tower after her son, Lord Darnley's, betrothal to Mary, Queen of Scots was announced (1566)
21 Edward VI's councillors signed Letters Patent disinheriting his half-sisters, Mary and Elizabeth, and naming Jane Grey his heir (1553)
22 Bernardino de Silva, Spanish ambassador, had his first audience with Elizabeth (1564)
23 Elizabeth wrote to Mary, Queen of Scots, admonishing her for marrying the Earl of Bothwell (1567)
24 Elizabeth dined with Lord Robert Dudley in London on his 29th birthday (1561)
25 Elizabeth thanked the Earl and Countess of Shrewsbury for guarding Mary, Queen of Scots (1577)
26 Thomas Young, Archbishop of York, died (1568)
27 Elizabeth awarded a royal charter to Jesus College, Oxford (1571)
28 Henry VIII was born at Greenwich Palace (1491)
29 Thomas Boleyn, Earl of Wiltshire, stripped of his office of Lord Privy Seal (1536)
30 Henri II of France was mortally wounded in a jousting match (1559)

Birthdays	Anniversaries	Reminders	Projects

Gardening	Events	Occasions	Festivals

THE VISIT OF THE DUKE OF ANJOU

From her accession, Elizabeth was pressed to marry and numerous suitors were suggested by her ministers. Elizabeth was reluctant to marry at all and she played one candidate off against another for many years, enjoying the game of courtship.

The closest she came to marrying for political reasons was in the 1570s, when the French prince, François, Duke of Anjou, was put forward. He was only 16, to Elizabeth's thirty-nine, but she took up the idea with enthusiasm, an alliance with France to counter the growing power of Spain being English policy. Initial talks collapsed after the Massacre of St Bartholomew that saw the murder of thousands of French Huguenots.

In 1578, as part of a French campaign to destablilise Spanish rule in the Netherlands, a policy with which Elizabeth's ministers heartily concurred, the match with Anjou was revived, although the English were wary of Anjou's real motives and Walsingham thought his only intent was to flatter Elizabeth into accepting French encroachment in the Netherlands. In 1579, Anjou's envoy, M. Simier, arrived in London to woo Elizabeth by proxy. Elizabeth was so enchanted by his gallantries that her ministers talked darkly of love potions. Before committing herself, Elizabeth insisted

on seeing Anjou, who agreed to visit that summer. The prince proved witty and charming, and Elizabeth enjoyed the heady delights of a whirlwind romance, declaring that she had never met anyone more agreeable to her. But Elizabeth's ministers, who had once urged the queen to marry, now backtracked – she was too old to risk childbirth and he was too French, and too Catholic, to be acceptable. Elizabeth decided to press ahead, agreeing that Anjou could practise his religion in private after their marriage, but stipulating that she needed time to talk her council round. Simier departed, confident of having achieved his aims. With both men gone, Elizabeth reverted to her old game of encouragement without commitment. The matter limped along until 1581, when the alliance again seemed desirable. Anjou returned to England, and Elizabeth seemed as infatuated as before. She publicly declared that she would marry him, although the terms she sent to France were so one-sided that there was no possibility of agreement. Nevertheless, Anjou clung on, not agreeing to leave until Elizabeth lent him money for the Netherlands campaign. She affected great sorrow at his departure, and the match was not finally scotched until Anjou's death in 1584.

SOMERSET PLACE

Somerset Place was Elizabeth's first official London residence. Its location on the Strand was a convenient point on the processional route between the Tower of London and Westminster.

Originally granted Durham Place in Henry VIII's will, Elizabeth was persuaded by the Duke of Northumberland to exchange it for Somerset Place, which she came into possession of in 1553. Edward Seymour, Duke of Somerset, had begun building Somerset Place during the Protectorate of his nephew, Edward VI. It was only partially constructed when Somerset fell from his mighty position and was executed. Consequently, it required substantial work, mostly on the interiors, to complete it for use by Elizabeth.

In July 1553, Elizabeth came to Somerset Place from Hatfield House, with her 2,000 mounted and armed attendants dressed in Tudor green and white livery, after her half-sister Mary had successfully claimed the Crown. It became the focus of her power base in the months leading up to Mary's death in 1558 and, following a brief stop at the Tower of London, was where she initially stayed in London when she became queen. Elizabeth held her first London-based Privy Council meetings in the Great Council Chamber, hosting 15 in total there before she moved into Whitehall Palace, which, as monarch, became her official London residence.

However, Elizabeth retained Somerset Place and used it primarily for hosting foreign ambassadors, and provided lodgings for some senior nobles there too. Her first cousin, Henry Carey, Baron Hunsdon, had a suite of privy lodgings at Somerset Place and used it as his London base before he bought his own residence at Blackfriars.

Elizabeth continued to use Somerset Place from time to time. She made 14 visits to it during her reign, often as part of a procession or for an important public event. In 1585 she spent Lent there and heard her Lenten sermons sitting at a window in the outer court, where she was seen by crowds of people.

After Elizabeth's death, James VI & I granted it to his wife, Anne of Denmark, and it remained the official London residence of queens consort throughout the seventeenth century. In the eighteenth century, the Government demolished what had become the old-fashioned and dilapidated Tudor palace, replacing it with the impressive Neo-Classical building which remains at the heart of Somerset House today. Now it is operated by Somerset House Trust as a public working arts centre.

JUNE

1 Anne Boleyn, pregnant with
Elizabeth, was crowned
Queen of England (1533)

2 Thomas Howard, 4th Duke
of Norfolk, was executed for
treason (1572)

3 Earl of Essex's expedition
left England for Cadiz,
Spain (1596)

4 Elizabeth wrote to Earl and
Countess of Shrewsbury,
joking about Earl of
Leicester's new eating
regime (1577)

5 Anne Cecil, Countess of
Oxford, daughter of Sir
William Cecil, died (1588)

6 Robert Cecil, son of
Sir William Cecil, was
baptised (1563)

JUNE

7   Roderigo Lopez was
executed for allegedly trying
to poison Elizabeth (1594)

8   Elizabeth stayed with
Sir Thomas Gresham at
Osterley, Middlesex (1571)

9   Thomas Radcliffe, 3rd Earl
of Sussex, died (1583)

10 François, Duke of Anjou, Elizabeth's last serious suitor, died (1584)

11 St Barnabas the Apostle's Day

Marie of Guise, Queen and Regent of Scotland, died (1560)

12 Lord Deputy and Council of Ireland excused themselves to Elizabeth after granting Edward Fitton a pardon for murder (1573)

JUNE

13 Final night of Elizabeth's
    eight-day stay at Hatfield
    Palace (1575)

14 Thomas Wharton, 2nd
    Baron Wharton, died (1572)

15 Elizabeth Knollys was born
    (1549)

16 Lady Russell and Lord Cobham entertained Elizabeth at Blackfriars (1600)

17 Edward VI altered his 'Devise for the Succession' to leave the throne to Lady Jane Grey (1553)

18 Robert Devereux, 2nd Earl of Essex, succeeded his stepfather, Leicester, as Master of the Horse (1587)

JUNE

19 James VI & I, Elizabeth's
successor, was born (1566)

20 Countess of Lennox sent to
Tower after her son, Lord
Darnley's, betrothal to
Mary, Queen of Scots was
announced (1566)

21 Edward VI's councillors
signed Letters Patent
disinheriting his half-sisters,
Mary and Elizabeth, and
naming Jane Grey his heir
(1553)

22 Bernardino de Silva,
Spanish ambassador, had
his first audience with
Elizabeth (1564)

23 Elizabeth wrote to
Mary, Queen of Scots,
admonishing her for
marrying the Earl of
Bothwell (1567)

24 **St John the Baptist's Day**

Elizabeth dined with Lord
Robert Dudley in London
on his 29th birthday (1561)

JUNE

25 Elizabeth thanked Earl and Countess of Shrewsbury for guarding Mary, Queen of Scots (1577)

26 Thomas Young, Archbishop of York, died (1568)

27 Elizabeth awarded a royal charter to Jesus College, Oxford (1571)

28 Henry VIII was born at
Greenwich Palace (1491)

29 **Feast of SS Peter and Paul,
the Apostles**

Thomas Boleyn, Earl of
Wiltshire, was stripped of
his office of Lord Privy
Seal (1536)

30 Henri II of France was
mortally wounded in a
jousting match (1559)

JUNE

Notes

Notes

MONTH PLANNER

July

1 Parliament declared Henry VIII's daughters, Mary and Elizabeth, illegitimate (1536)

2 Sir Thomas Wentworth was indicted for treason for the loss of Calais (1558)

3 Elizabeth ate aboard the *Elizabeth Jonas*, her new warship, at Woolwich (1559)

4 William Byrd, composer and Gentleman of the Chapel Royal, died (1623)

5 Elizabeth visited Sir Richard Sackville and was entertained by a play and masque (1564)

6 Edward VI died, aged 15 (1553)

7 Elizabeth and her court attended a tournament at Greenwich (1560)

8 Mary I proclaimed queen at Kenninghall, in Norfolk (1553)

9 Elizabeth began her 19-day stay at Kenilworth Castle, guest of Earl of Leicester (1575)

10 Lady Jane Grey was proclaimed queen in London (1553)

11 Elizabeth stayed at Charterhouse, London, guest of Lord North (1561)

12 Henry VIII married his sixth wife, Katherine Parr (1543)

13 John Dee, astrologer and adviser to Elizabeth, was born (1527)

14 Elizabeth visited Dover as part of her summer progress through Kent (1573)

15 Inigo Jones, architect and theatre designer, was born (1573)

16 Anne of Cleves, Henry VIII's fourth wife, died (1557)

17 Elizabeth stayed at Osterley, Middlesex, guest of Sir Thomas Gresham (1570)

18 Katherine Astley, Elizabeth's governess, died (1565)

19 Privy Council proclaimed Mary queen (1553)

20 Elizabeth stayed at Cobham Hall, Kent, guest of Lord Cobham (1559)

21 John Dudley, Duke of Northumberland, was arrested for his role in placing Lady Jane Grey on the throne (1553)

22 Elizabeth stayed with Lord Burghley at Theobalds, Hertfordshire (1572)

23 Henry Carey, 1st Baron Hunsdon died (1596)

24 Scottish lords forced Mary, Queen of Scots to abdicate (1567)

25 Elizabeth wrote letter rebuking the Polish ambassador for his insolence to her (1597)

26 Last day of Elizabeth's six-day stay with Earl of Sussex at New Hall, Essex (1561)

27 Thomas Knyvett, Gentleman of the Privy Chamber, was buried (1622)

28 Henry VIII married his fifth wife, Katheryn Howard (1540)

29 Elizabeth rode into London with ceremonial escort of 2,000 armed retainers (1553)

30 French ambassadors renewed the Duke of Anjou's suit for marriage to Elizabeth (1578)

31 Elizabeth wrote a letter in Italian to her stepmother, Katherine Parr (1544)

Birthdays	Anniversaries	Reminders	Projects

Gardening	Events	Occasions	Festivals

THE KENILWORTH REVELS

In 1575, Robert Dudley, Earl of Leicester, arranged the most magnificent entertainment of Elizabeth's reign, spending a reputed £60,000 on a glorious spectacle intended to charm the queen and woo her into acceptance of his long-pressed suit for her hand. Elizabeth's summer progress brought her to Kenilworth by 9th July and she was greeted at the castle gates by one of the ten Sybils (prophets in Ancient Roman lore), who prognosticated long life for her.

A porter, dressed as Hercules, offered her the keys to the castle. Once inside, the procession entered the tilt-yard, where another speech of welcome and adulation from the Lady of the Lake caressed Elizabeth's ears. A short bridge decorated with fruit, flowers and musical instruments led to the inner court, where Elizabeth dismounted, music playing all the while.

After church the next day, the company danced and enjoyed a firework display. Monday was so hot that Elizabeth remained indoors until five, when she emerged to go hunting. On her return, she was met by a 'wild man' who appeared overcome by the apparition of the mysterious beauty and conversed, in rather lame verse, with 'Echo', about her identity. After he discovered the lovely woman was none other than the queen, he implied that, since Leicester had

showered so many gifts of love on her, he ought to be loved in return.

The Lady of the Lake reappeared in a tableau, whose purport was that the Lady had been harassed by Sir Bruce Sans Pitie, who pursued her in revenge for his cousin, Merlin (whom the Lady had entombed). Neptune had taken pity on her, and surrounded her with waves to keep her safe. She could only be rescued by a better woman than herself. Elizabeth's presence set the Lady free, after which the sea god, Proteus, appeared, riding a dolphin.

Tuesday was devoted to dancing, followed by a walk in the park. Hunting was Wednesday's pleasure, then on Thursday, there was a bear-baiting. Less bloodthirsty was the Italian acrobat.

Friday and Saturday were plagued with storms, but Sunday saw performances from the local populace, including morris dancing, tilting at the quintain and scenes from the story of Robin Hood and Maid Marian, including a country bridal, intended to make Elizabeth long for matrimony.

Elizabeth departed after 19 days. She had not succumbed to Leicester's suit, but the revels at Kenilworth remained unequalled in either beauty or cost.

116

KENILWORTH CASTLE

The vast and mighty Kenilworth Castle had been a favoured and prestigious royal castle over several centuries before Elizabeth gave it to Robert Dudley in 1563.

The original 12th century Norman keep, which still stands today, has been supplemented by an enormous mere (man-made lake) and large hunting park, along with additional buildings, all constructed of the local red sandstone, over subsequent centuries.

In the fourteenth century, John of Gaunt, son of Edward III, acquired this Lancastrian stronghold through his first wife, Blanche of Lancaster. Inspired by his father's work at Windsor Castle, John undertook substantial building works, turning the great fortress into a luxurious royal residence. The magnificent Great Hall he created, approached up a massive set of stairs, with a hammer beam roof and cathedral-like windows, was of a similar scale and design to the Great Halls at Windsor Castle and Westminster.

Kenilworth Castle was also a favoured residence of both Henry VII, who visited regularly, and Henry VIII, who built a timber range, closing the inner ward to the east, there.

Robert Dudley remodelled the castle extensively and created a new suite of privy lodgings in a large four-storey tower for Elizabeth's use. Within the tower, above Elizabeth's bedchamber and closets, was another floor, containing an ante chamber and dancing gallery, with extensive windows on three sides. Elizabeth made four visits to Kenilworth, the most famous of which was her 19-day stay as part of the 1575 summer progress. Dudley, now Earl of Leicester, spent enormous sums of money on an extravaganza of entertainment: music, feasts, dancing, plays, pageants, hunting, bear-baiting and fireworks. This is in addition to what he spent on developing a privy garden for the visit, with a bejewelled aviary, raised terrace walk, marble fountain, obelisks and colourful, abundant planting. Leicester's Elizabethan garden is long gone, but luckily English Heritage has recreated it on the same site.

Kenilworth Castle was partially destroyed on the orders of Parliament in 1649, after the Civil War. Leicester's Gatehouse and the Tudor stables remain intact and they, along with the castle's substantial ruins, can be visited today. New staircases and viewing platforms recently installed by English Heritage make it possible to stand at the top of Leicester's ruined tower and look out over the mere and surrounding countryside, much as Elizabeth would have done some 450 years ago.

July

1   Parliament declared Henry
VIII's daughters, Mary
and Elizabeth, illegitimate
(1536)

2   Sir Thomas Wentworth was
indicted for treason for the
loss of Calais (1558)

3   Elizabeth ate aboard the
Elizabeth Jonas, her new
warship, at Woolwich (1559)

4   William Byrd, composer
     and Gentleman of the
     Chapel Royal, died (1623)

5   Elizabeth visited Sir
     Richard Sackville and was
     entertained by a play and
     masque (1564)

6   Edward VI died, aged 15
     (1553)

JULY

7   Elizabeth and her court
attended a tournament at
Greenwich (1560)

8   Mary I proclaimed queen
at Kenninghall, in Norfolk
(1553)

9   Elizabeth began her 19-day
stay at Kenilworth Castle,
guest of Earl of Leicester
(1575)

10 Lady Jane Grey was
proclaimed queen in
London (1553)

11 Elizabeth stayed at
Charterhouse, London, the
guest of Lord North (1561)

12 Henry VIII married his
sixth wife, Katherine Parr
(1543)

JULY

13 John Dee, astrologer and
adviser to Elizabeth, was
born (1527)

14 Elizabeth visited Dover as
part of her summer progress
through Kent (1573)

15 Inigo Jones, architect and
theatre designer, was born
(1573)

16 Anne of Cleves, Henry VIII's fourth wife, died (1557)

17 Elizabeth stayed at Osterley, Middlesex, guest of Sir Thomas Gresham (1570)

18 Katherine Astley, Elizabeth's governess, died (1565)

JULY

19 Privy Council proclaimed
Mary queen (1553)

_____

_____

_____

_____

_____

_____

_____

_____

20 Elizabeth stayed at Cobham
Hall, Kent, guest of Lord
Cobham (1559)

_____

_____

_____

_____

_____

_____

_____

21 John Dudley, Duke of
Northumberland, was
arrested for his role in
placing Lady Jane Grey on
the throne (1553)

_____

_____

_____

_____

_____

_____

22 **St Mary Magdalene's Day**

Elizabeth stayed with Lord
Burghley at Theobalds,
Hertfordshire (1572)

23 Henry Carey, 1st Baron
Hunsdon, Elizabeth's first
cousin, died (1596)

24 Scottish lords forced Mary,
Queen of Scots to abdicate
(1567)

JULY

25 **St James the Apostle's Day**

Elizabeth wrote a letter
rebuking the Polish
ambassador for his insolence
to her (1597)

26 Last day of Elizabeth's six-
day stay with Earl of Sussex
at New Hall, Essex (1561)

27 Thomas Knyvett,
Gentleman of the Privy
Chamber, was buried (1622)

28 Henry VIII married his fifth wife, Katheryn Howard (1540)

29 Elizabeth rode into London with ceremonial escort of 2,000 armed retainers (1553)

30 French ambassadors renewed Duke of Anjou's suit for marriage to Elizabeth (1578)

July

31   Elizabeth wrote a letter in
Italian to her stepmother,
Katherine Parr (1544)

Notes

Notes

MONTH PLANNER

August

1 Sir John Astley, Gentleman of the Privy Chamber, died (1596)

2 Spanish forces landed at Mount's Bay and sacked several Cornish towns (1595)

3 Mary I entered London as queen (1553)

4 Sir William Cecil, Lord Burghley, Elizabeth's chief councillor, died (1598)

5 First day of Elizabeth's five-day visit to Cambridge (1564)

6 Elizabeth visited Earl and Countess of Essex at Chartley (1578)

7 Elizabeth delivered impromptu Latin oration at Cambridge University (1564)

8 Elizabeth stayed with the Bishop of Winchester at Farnham (1560)

9 Elizabeth delivered 'Armada' speech to troops at Tilbury, Essex (1588)

10 Last day of Elizabeth's five-day stay at Nonsuch Palace, as guest of Earl of Arundel (1559)

11 First day of Elizabeth's four-day stay in Suffolk with William Waldegrave (1561)

12 Lady Katherine Grey was sent to Tower of London after her secret marriage (1561)

13 Sir Humphrey Radcliffe, MP, died (1566)

14 Irish forces defeated the English at the Battle of Yellow Ford (1598)

15 Mary Shelton, Lady Scudamore, one of Elizabeth's sleeping companions, was buried (1603)

16 Elizabeth began a six-day stay with Earl of Oxford in Essex (1561)

17 François, Duke of Anjou, arrived incognito at Greenwich for 11-day courtship of Elizabeth (1579)

18 News of Throckmorton Plot reached court (1583)

19 Mary, Queen of Scots returned to Scotland to begin her personal rule (1561)

20 Sir William Cavendish and Elizabeth (Bess) Hardwick were married (1547)

21 Elizabeth appointed former Jesuit Christopher Perkins as her Latin secretary (1601)

22 Thomas Percy, 7th Earl of Northumberland, was executed (1572)

23 Massacre of St Bartholomew's Day began in Paris (1572)

24 Thomas Howard, 1st Earl of Suffolk, was born (1561)

25 Lady Katherine Grey was born (1540)

26 Robert Devereux, 2nd Earl of Essex, was released from house arrest (1600)

27 Russian ambassador Andrea Gregorowitz Saviena arrived in London (1569)

28 Elizabeth was in Bristol to ratify the Treaty of Bristol with Spain (1574)

29 Elizabeth hunted in Windsor Forest with French ambassador Michel de Castelnau (1584)

30 George Gower, Elizabeth's Serjeant Painter, died (1596)

31 Elizabeth left Woodstock for her stay in Oxford (1566)

Birthdays	Anniversaries	Reminders	Projects

Gardening	Events	Occasions	Festivals

THE SPANISH ARMADA

On the death of Elizabeth's half-sister, Mary I, her widower, Philip II of Spain, suggested that the Anglo-Spanish alliance should be maintained by them marrying. Elizabeth did not definitely reject him, but it was soon apparent she would not accept the offer. Over the years, the once strong alliance broke down, foundering on the religious divide between Catholic Spain and an England that was moving steadily towards Protestantism. When the Netherlands, part of Philip's inheritance, broke out in revolt for a mixture of religious and political causes, Elizabeth was called on to support fellow Protestants. Despite the urging of her government, Elizabeth was reluctant to allow England to be involved – she did not wish to undermine Philip's sovereignty, she was not in sympathy with the Calvinist religion of parts of the Netherlands, and, most importantly, she could not afford a war.

Throughout the 1570s and early 1580s, England gave the Netherlands limited support. Meanwhile, plots in favour of Mary, Queen of Scots continued to spring up, and eventually the Scottish queen was executed. This, together with her support for his Netherlandish rebels, the actions of English shipping in harassing the Spanish fleet as it brought treasure from the Americas and the burning of the Spanish fleet in Cadiz by Francis Drake, led Philip to declare war.

He amassed an armada, which was sent forth in the summer of 1588 with the objective of meeting the army of his general, the Duke of Parma, in the Netherlands, to transport an army to invade and conquer England. The armada was led by the loyal but amateur Duke of Medina Sidonia, whilst the English fleet was under the command of the very experienced Lord Howard of Effingham. The English ships were more manoeuvrable and the strategy of setting fireships amongst the Spanish at anchor in Calais extremely effective. The armada was defeated, through a combination of excellent English seamanship and unseasonably foul weather which blew both fleets north. The English, out of ammunition and supplies, ceased pursuit at the Firth of Forth, but the Scottish king refused succour to the Spanish, and the majority of the armada was wrecked along the coasts of the British Isles.

The war ground on until the end of Elizabeth's reign, but in retrospect this was the high-water mark of her rule. Her image as Gloriana, defeating the enemy and safeguarding Protestant England, was forever enshrined in the memory of the English.

SUDELEY CASTLE

The picturesque Sudeley Castle, built of honey-coloured Cotswold stone and nestling in the rolling Gloucestershire countryside, has strong connections with the Tudor royal family. Elizabeth's step-mother, Henry VIII's sixth wife, Queen Katherine Parr, is buried within its grounds.

The castle first came into the hands of the Crown during the reign of the Yorkist king Edward IV. He granted it to his younger brother, Richard, Duke of Gloucester, who undertook extensive renovations to the castle created by the Lancastrian Sir Ralph de Boteler and built the east range and great Tithe Barn, both of which are now romantic ruins.

Henry VIII and Anne Boleyn stayed at Sudeley for a week during their long summer progress of 1535 and it is during this time that Thomas Cromwell, who accompanied them, began work on what would become the Dissolution of the Monasteries.

Edward VI granted Sudeley to his uncle, Sir Thomas Seymour, who brought his pregnant wife, Dowager Queen Katherine Parr, and ward, Lady Jane Grey, here in the summer of 1548. Sadly, Katherine died within days of giving birth to their daughter. She was buried in the chapel adjacent to the castle in what is now the restored St Mary's Church, where her Victorian tomb can be visited still.

Mary I gave Sudeley to Sir John Brydges, 1st Baron Chandos. He had been Lieutenant of the Tower during the early part of her reign and thus had had custody of Lady Jane Grey, Sir Thomas Wyatt and Elizabeth herself, amongst others. His family undertook substantial alterations and repairs to the castle during the 1570s.

Elizabeth stayed at Sudeley on her summer progresses of 1574 and 1575. She made a third visit on the 1592 progress to commemorate the anniversary of the defeat of the Spanish Armada. Huge preparations were made for the three-day party held on this visit, involving the creation of substantial and spectacular gardens with water features and a banqueting house. Archaeological digs in 2018 and 2019 uncovered evidence of these gardens, including the possible remains of the banqueting house.

Much of the castle that survives today is from the sixteenth century rebuilding by the Chandos family, with the Dent family's Victorian restoration. A number of rooms are open to the public, with a series of exhibitions that include books and hand-written letters of Katherine Parr's, along with replica Tudor costumes. Sudeley's extensive grounds include the Queens' Garden, built on what was the Tudor parterre to commemorate the four queens who have stayed at Sudeley.

AUGUST

1   Sir John Astley, Gentleman of the Privy Chamber, died (1596)

2   Spanish forces landed at Mount's Bay and sacked several Cornish towns (1595)

3   Mary I entered London as queen (1553)

4   Sir William Cecil, Lord
Burghley, Elizabeth's chief
councillor, died (1598)

5   First day of Elizabeth's
five-day visit to Cambridge
(1564)

6   Elizabeth, visited Earl
and Countess of Essex at
Chartley (1578)

AUGUST

7   Elizabeth delivered
impromptu Latin oration
at Cambridge University
(1564)

8   Elizabeth stayed with the
Bishop of Winchester at
Farnham (1560)

9   Elizabeth delivered
'Armada' speech to troops at
Tilbury, Essex (1588)

AUGUST

10 Last day of Elizabeth's five-
day stay at Nonsuch Palace,
as guest of Earl of Arundel
(1559)

11 First day of Elizabeth's
four-day stay in Suffolk
with William Waldegrave
(1561)

12 Lady Katherine Grey was
sent to Tower of London
after her secret marriage
(1561)

AUGUST

13 Sir Humphrey Radcliffe,
MP, died (1566)

14 Irish forces defeated the
English at the Battle of
Yellow Ford (1598)

15 Mary Shelton, Lady
Scudamore, one of
Elizabeth's sleeping
companions, was buried
(1603)

16 Elizabeth began a six-day
stay with Earl of Oxford in
Essex (1561)

17 François, Duke of Anjou,
arrived incognito at
Greenwich for 11-day
courtship of Elizabeth
(1579)

18 News of the Throckmorton
Plot reached court (1583)

AUGUST

19 Mary, Queen of Scots
returned to Scotland to
begin her personal rule
(1561)

20 Sir William Cavendish and
Elizabeth (Bess) Hardwick
were married (1547)

21 Elizabeth appointed former
Jesuit Christopher Perkins
as her Latin secretary (1601)

22 Thomas Percy, 7th Earl
of Northumberland, was
executed (1572)

_____

_____

_____

_____

_____

_____

_____

_____

_____

23 Massacre of St
Bartholomew's Day began
in Paris (1572)

_____

_____

_____

_____

_____

_____

_____

_____

24 **St Bartholomew the
Apostle's Day**

Thomas Howard, 1st Earl
of Suffolk, was born (1561)

_____

_____

_____

_____

_____

_____

_____

AUGUST

25 Lady Katherine Grey was born (1540)

_____
_____
_____
_____
_____
_____
_____
_____

26 Robert Devereux, 2nd Earl of Essex, was released from house arrest (1600)

_____
_____
_____
_____
_____
_____
_____

27 Russian ambassador Andrea Gregorowitz Saviena arrived in London (1569)

_____
_____
_____
_____
_____
_____
_____

28 Elizabeth was in Bristol to
ratify the Treaty of Bristol
with Spain (1574)

29 Elizabeth hunted in
Windsor Forest with
French ambassador Michel
de Castelnau (1584)

30 George Gower, Elizabeth's
Serjeant Painter, died
(1596)

AUGUST

31 Elizabeth left Woodstock
for her stay in Oxford (1566)

Notes

Notes

MONTH PLANNER

September

1   Anne Boleyn was created Lady Marquis of Pembroke (1532)

2   News of a conspiracy in Lancashire to free Mary, Queen of Scots reached court (1570)

3   Elizabeth visited Wingham in Kent (1573)

4   Robert Dudley, Earl of Leicester, died (1588)

5   Katherine Parr, Dowager Queen of England, died (1548)

6   Sir Henry Jerningham, Privy Councillor, died (1572)

7   Elizabeth was born at Greenwich (1533)

8   Amy Robsart, Lady Dudley, died in mysterious circumstances (1560)

9   Mary, Queen of Scots was crowned (1543)

10 Elizabeth was christened (1533)

11 Sir Thomas Tresham the Younger died (1605)

12 First day of Elizabeth's two-day stay at Newbury, Berkshire (1568)

13 Philip II, King of Spain, died (1598)

14 Earl of Bedford warned Cecil of French warships approaching Ireland (1570)

15 Elizabeth issued a warrant permitting the torture of two of the Duke of Norfolk's servants (1571)

16 Russian ambassador arrived at court, seeking a wife for Ivan the Terrible (1573)

17 Elizabeth reported to be so grieved by Leicester's death, she had locked herself into her room (1588)

18 Last day of Elizabeth's three-day stay at Faversham, Kent (1573)

19 Katherine Willoughby, Duchess of Suffolk, died (1580)

20 Treaty of Hampton Court signed with Huguenot leaders (1562)

21 Robert Dudley, Earl of Leicester, married Lettice Knollys (1578)

22 Sir Philip Sidney was wounded at the Battle of Zutphen (1586)

23 Katherine Pole, Countess of Huntingdon, died (1571)

24 Edward Seymour, Viscount Beauchamp, was born in Tower of London (1561)

25 Mary, Queen of Scots was moved to Fotheringhay Castle, Northamptonshire (1586)

26 Francis Drake arrived at Plymouth, following his circumnavigation of globe (1580)

27 Michael Heneage, politician and antiquary, was born (1540)

28 Robert Devereux, Earl of Essex, burst into Elizabeth's bedchamber unannounced (1599)

29 Lord Robert Dudley was created Earl of Leicester (1564)

30 Cecilia of Sweden's son, Elizabeth's godson, was christened at English court (1565)

Birthdays	Anniversaries	Reminders	Projects

Gardening	Events	Occasions	Festivals

BIRTH AND CHRISTENING

On 26th August 1533, Queen Anne Boleyn retired for her first childbirth. The location selected for what the queen and her husband, Henry VIII, fondly assumed would be the birth of a son was the palace of Greenwich, where Henry himself had been born.

The protocol surrounding royal childbirth was complex and, in modern terms, unhealthy. Nevertheless, on 7th September, around three in the afternoon, Anne was safely delivered. As soon as the news was heard, a Te Deum was sung at St Paul's. In accordance with custom, the queen sent out letters announcing the birth – an 's' hastily added to the pre-prepared text announcing the birth of a prince. The child was healthy, and the disappointment of her sex was quickly overcome – at least for public consumption. The christening took place three days later.

The procession formed up in the Great Hall of the palace and walked along a carpet of rushes, between tapestry hangings, to the adjacent church of the Friars Observant, also hung with arras. The attendees consisted of the king's council, the members of his chapel, dressed in their copes, and a panoply of barons, bishops and noblemen, as well as the Lord Mayor, the aldermen and 40 of the chief citizens of London. The king's cousin, Henry, Marquis of Exeter, carried a taper of wax; another cousin, the Marquis of Dorset, held the salt and the Earl of Essex bore the gilt basins, whilst Anne's cousin, Lady Mary Howard, daughter of the Duke of Norfolk, carried the chrism. The baby, wrapped in a long mantle of purple velvet, was in the arms of Agnes, Dowager-duchess of Norfolk, who was to be one of the godmothers, alongside the Marchioness of Dorset. Anne's father, the Earl of Wiltshire, along with two other nobles, followed Agnes, holding up the velvet train. Four men, including Anne's brother, Lord Rochford, supported a canopy over the infant. Inside the church, a cloth was draped over the silver christening font, and above it was suspended a canopy of crimson satin, fringed with gold.

The ceremony was led by the Bishop of London. Thomas Cranmer, Archbishop of Canterbury, was godfather, and the baby was named Elizabeth – after both of her grandmothers. Immediately after the christening, Elizabeth was confirmed, her godmother for this ceremony being the Marchioness of Exeter. Trumpets were blown and the procession, lit by 500 torches, returned to the palace.

GREENWICH PALACE

Elizabeth was born at Greenwich Palace, as was her older half-sister, Mary. It was Elizabeth's favourite residence, and, after the Palace of Whitehall, it was the one she used most frequently.

Greenwich Palace was built by Elizabeth's grandfather, Henry VII, around 1500. Located on the River Thames, down river from the city of London, this new palace was built on the site of an earlier 'pleasuance' manor created for Humphrey, Duke of Gloucester, in the fifteenth century. It was highly innovative in its design, the first royal palace to be built and decorated so extensively in brick. The principal range running parallel to, and facing, the river had bay windows looking both ways. This range also featured a huge integrated five-storey tower, containing studies, libraries and other private rooms above the king's privy chamber and bedchamber.

Henry VIII spent a great deal of time at Greenwich in the first half of his reign. The palace became his principal residence between 1512, when the Palace of Westminster was damaged by fire, and 1532, when the Palace of Whitehall was completed. He built stables, an armoury and a large tiltyard for jousting, with an adjacent four-storey permanent viewing grandstand. It was at Greenwich, in May

1536, whilst watching a game of real tennis, that Queen Anne Boleyn was arrested and taken by river to the Tower of London. Greenwich was also the venue for Henry's wedding to his fourth wife, Anne of Cleves.

Elizabeth tended to visit Greenwich in the summer months and when in residence she occupied the king's apartments on the riverfront. Here she had an official 'standing' bedchamber and a private one beyond that. Robert Dudley, Earl of Leicester, also had lodgings in the main riverfront range, close to the queen, as, indeed, he had in every royal house. Elizabeth enjoyed picnicking and sitting in the extensive gardens at Greenwich. In 1589 a 'great seat' was made under her favourite mulberry tree; it had a brick base, a seat covered in lead and four pillars to support a canopy.

Most of Greenwich Palace was demolished during the Commonwealth. In the 1690s, a hospital for seamen was built on the site and in the 1800s it became the Royal Naval College. Today, it is possible to see some remnants of the excavated palace walls, situated beneath the Painted Hall at the Old Royal Naval College.

SEPTEMBER

1   Anne Boleyn was created
Lady Marquis of Pembroke
(1532)

2   News of a conspiracy in
Lancashire to free Mary,
Queen of Scots reached
court (1570)

3   Elizabeth visited Wingham
in Kent (1573)

4   Robert Dudley, Earl of
Leicester, died (1588)

5   Katherine Parr, Dowager
Queen of England, died
(1548)

6   Sir Henry Jerningham,
Privy Councillor, died
(1572)

September

7 Elizabeth was born at
Greenwich (1533)

_____
_____
_____
_____
_____
_____
_____
_____
_____

8 Amy Robsart, Lady
Dudley, died in mysterious
circumstances (1560)

_____
_____
_____
_____
_____
_____
_____
_____

9 Mary, Queen of Scots was
crowned (1543)

_____
_____
_____
_____
_____
_____
_____
_____

10 Elizabeth was christened
(1533)

_____

_____

_____

_____

_____

_____

_____

_____

11 Sir Thomas Tresham the
Younger died (1605)

_____

_____

_____

_____

_____

_____

_____

_____

12 First day of Elizabeth's
two-day stay at Newbury,
Berkshire (1568)

_____

_____

_____

_____

_____

_____

_____

_____

SEPTEMBER

13   Philip II, King of Spain, died (1598)

14   Earl of Bedford warned Cecil of French warships approaching Ireland (1570)

15   Elizabeth issued a warrant permitting the torture of two of the Duke of Norfolk's servants (1571)

16 Russian ambassador arrived
at court, seeking a wife for
Ivan the Terrible (1573)

17 Elizabeth reported to be so
grieved by Leicester's death,
she had locked herself into
her room (1588)

18 Last day of Elizabeth's
three-day stay at
Faversham, Kent (1573)

SEPTEMBER

19 Katherine Willoughby, Duchess of Suffolk, died (1580)

20 Treaty of Hampton Court signed with Huguenot leaders (1562)

21 **St Matthew the Apostle's Day**

Robert Dudley, Earl of Leicester, married Lettice Knollys (1578)

22   Sir Philip Sidney was
wounded at Battle of
Zutphen (1586)

23   Katherine Pole, Countess of
Huntingdon, died (1571)

24   Edward Seymour, Viscount
Beauchamp, was born in
Tower of London (1561)

SEPTEMBER

25 Mary, Queen of Scots was
moved to Fotheringhay
Castle, Northamptonshire
(1586)

26 Francis Drake arrived at
Plymouth, following his
circumnavigation of the
globe (1580)

27 Michael Heneage, politician
and antiquary, was born
(1540)

28 Robert Devereux, Earl
of Essex, burst into
Elizabeth's bedchamber
unannounced (1599)

29 **Feast of St Michael and
All Angels (Michaelmas)**

Lord Robert Dudley was
created Earl of Leicester
(1564)

30 Cecilia of Sweden's son,
Elizabeth's godson, was
christened at English court
(1565)

SEPTEMBER

Notes

Notes

MONTH PLANNER

October

1   Mary I crowned Queen of England (1553)

2   Thomas Seymour was appointed a Gentleman of the Privy Chamber (1537)

3   Elizabeth met Dr John Dee at Richmond Palace (1580)

4   Henry Wriothesley, 2nd Earl of Southampton, died (1581)

5   Lord Burghley made a speech opposing Elizabeth's marriage to Duke of Anjou (1579)

6   Duke of Alva appointed Lieutenant of the Netherlands, stoking tension between Catholics and Protestants (1569)

7   Margaret Douglas, Countess of Lennox, born (1515)

8   Elizabeth stayed with Sir Francis Knollys at Rotherfield Greys, Oxfordshire (1576)

9   Elizabeth was guest of Sir Philip Boteler at Sunbury, Surrey (1600)

10   Elizabeth was taken ill with smallpox (1562)

11   Third night of Elizabeth's four-day stay at Windsor Castle (1576)

12   Edward VI was born (1537)

13   Sir Edward Waterhouse, Chancellor of the Exchequer for Ireland, died (1591)

14   Trial of Mary, Queen of Scots began (1586)

15   Philip Howard, 13th Earl of Arundel, died in Tower of London (1595)

16   Thomas Davies, Bishop of Asaph, died (1573)

17   Sir Philip Sidney, poet, courtier and soldier, died in the Netherlands (1586)

18   Northumberland's sons, John, Henry, Ambrose and Robert Dudley, released from Tower of London (1554)

19   Anthony Browne, 1st Viscount Montagu, died (1592)

20   Henri, Duke of Anjou, was suggested as a suitor for Elizabeth (1570)

21   Elizabeth stayed with Earl of Arundel at Nonsuch Palace (1574)

22   Henry Parker, 11th Baron Morley, died in exile (1577)

23   Charles Howard was created Earl of Nottingham (1597)

24   Edward Stanley, 3rd Earl of Derby and Privy Councillor, died (1572)

25   John Somerville travelled to London, planning to assassinate Elizabeth (1583)

26   Mildred Cooke, Lady Cecil, wrote that she had taken Mary, daughter of Sir Henry Sidney, into her household (1570)

27   Elizabeth wrote to her half-sister, Mary, apologising for a delay caused to one of Mary's servants (1552)

28   Thomas Causton, composer, died (1570)

29   Lord Mayor of London's Procession (1568)

30   Elizabeth refused to renew Earl of Essex's monopoly on import of sweet wines (1485)

31   Sir Nicholas Hare, Speaker of the House of Commons, died (1557)

Birthdays	Anniversaries	Reminders	Projects

Gardening	Events	Occasions	Festivals

SMALLPOX

On 10th October 1562, Elizabeth felt unwell. Foolishly, according to her courtiers, she took a bath, which they believed weakened her, making her vulnerable to infection. Within a few days it was clear that she had caught smallpox. At first, her symptoms were fever, debility and the loss of the power of speech. No spots had appeared, leading her physicians to believe that death was inevitable. The Privy Council hastily convened. There was only one question before them – if the queen died, who would succeed her?

There were several possible candidates, each with differing degrees of credibility in law, religion and personality. The Queen of Scots was the obvious candidate under common law, but her Catholicism and links to France made her unattractive to Elizabeth's ministers. Cecil advocated Lady Katherine Grey, sister of the Lady Jane Grey who had been promoted as queen on the death of Edward VI, who was the heir under Henry VIII's will. A third possibility was the Earl of Huntingdon, descendant of the York royal family. None of the candidates commanded any majority amongst the councillors. Meanwhile, the queen's cousin, Henry Carey, Lord Hunsdon, had summoned another doctor, a German physician named Dr Burcot. Burcot had Elizabeth, who was by now unconscious, wrapped in red flannel and brought close to the fire. After two hours, the queen woke up and had recovered her power of speech. Her councillors were admitted to the bedroom and immediately she was asked to name her successor. To their horror, she requested that her favourite, Lord Robert Dudley, should be appointed protector of the realm with an annual salary of £20,000. She assured them all that, although she loved Lord Robert, nothing improper had ever passed between them. Anxious not to distress her, the Council appeared to accede to her wishes. Fortunately for the peace of the kingdom, Elizabeth made a steady recovery. By 25th October she was well enough to attend to affairs of state, although her face was still inflamed and scabbed and she remained out of sight. Within a further week, the pox had disappeared, apparently leaving her unscarred – a remarkably lucky escape. Less fortunate than Elizabeth was her lady-in-waiting, Mary Dudley, Lady Sidney. Lady Sidney had nursed the queen devotedly and paid the price by contracting smallpox herself. She recovered but was terribly disfigured. Despite this brush with mortality, Elizabeth still refused to name a successor.

HAMPTON COURT PALACE

This much-visited red brick palace on the Thames has become an internationally recognised icon of the Tudor dynasty. It was Henry VIII's favoured country residence in the latter part of his reign and more of it survives today than of any other Tudor palace.

Cardinal Wolsey acquired Hampton Court, situated beside the River Thames and convenient to the king at nearby Richmond Palace, in 1514. He proceeded to turn the moated manor house into one of the largest and most spectacular houses in England, built in fashionable red brick and incorporating Renaissance influences from Europe. In late 1528, Wolsey surrendered Hampton Court to Henry VIII, who then spent the next decade in further substantial building works, the pinnacle of which is the Great Hall, and its stunning hammer-beam roof, that can still be seen today.

Hampton Court remained a popular palace with all of Henry VIII's children, and Elizabeth spent a great deal of time there in the early years of her reign. However, it was at Hampton Court in 1562 that Elizabeth fell seriously ill with smallpox, and following this life-threatening event, and its unpleasant memories, she did not return for five years. Nonetheless, by the 1570s Elizabeth had reverted to regular visits and Hampton Court remained one of her most frequently visited country residences, after Greenwich and Richmond.

In her later years, Elizabeth showed great interest in gardens and those at Hampton Court were extensive and magnificent. Covering over 60 acres, they included formal gardens with topiary, a banqueting house and fish ponds, as laid out by Henry VIII in the 1530s. In Elizabeth's privy garden, wooden posts topped with heraldic beasts and low-level rails painted in white and green chevrons, were used to divide the space into squares, some filled with red brick-dust, others with white sand or green lawn, creating a chess board effect. Today, the Tudor Garden in the Chapel Court provides a glimpse of what this would have looked like.

Following Elizabeth's death, Hampton Court remained relatively unchanged and was little used by James VI & I and the Stuart kings. William III and Mary II had plans to re-build Hampton Court but lack of funds meant they were only partially implemented. In the 1830s, Queen Victoria opened Hampton Court Palace to the public. Today it is managed by Historic Royal Palaces on behalf of the Crown and receives some four million visits per year.

OCTOBER

1   Mary I crowned Queen of
England (1553)

_____

_____

_____

_____

_____

_____

_____

_____

2   Thomas Seymour was
appointed a Gentleman of
the Privy Chamber (1537)

_____

_____

_____

_____

_____

_____

_____

_____

3   Elizabeth met Dr John Dee
at Richmond Palace (1580)

_____

_____

_____

_____

_____

_____

_____

_____

4 Henry Wriothesley, 2nd
Earl of Southampton, died
(1581)

5 Lord Burghley made
speech opposing Elizabeth's
marriage to Duke of Anjou
(1579)

6 **St Luke the Evangelist's
Day**

Duke of Alva appointed
Lieutenant of the
Netherlands, stoking
tension between Catholics
and Protestants (1569)

OCTOBER

7 Margaret Douglas,
Countess of Lennox, born
(1515)

_____
_____
_____
_____
_____
_____
_____
_____
_____

8 Elizabeth stayed with
Sir Francis Knollys
at Rotherfield Greys,
Oxfordshire (1576)

_____
_____
_____
_____
_____
_____
_____
_____

9 Elizabeth was guest of Sir
Philip Boteler at Sunbury,
Surrey (1600)

_____
_____
_____
_____
_____
_____
_____
_____

10   Elizabeth was taken ill with
smallpox (1562)

11   Third night of Elizabeth's
four-day stay at Windsor
Castle (1576)

12   Edward VI was born (1537)

OCTOBER

13 Sir Edward Waterhouse, Chancellor of the Exchequer for Ireland, died (1591)

14 Trial of Mary, Queen of Scots began (1586)

15 Philip Howard, 13th Earl of Arundel, died in Tower of London (1595)

16 Thomas Davies, Bishop of
Asaph, died (1573)

_____

_____

_____

_____

_____

_____

_____

_____

_____

17 Sir Philip Sidney, poet,
courtier and soldier, died in
the Netherlands (1586)

_____

_____

_____

_____

_____

_____

_____

_____

18 Northumberland's sons,
John, Henry, Ambrose and
Robert Dudley, released
from Tower of London
(1554)

_____

_____

_____

_____

_____

_____

_____

OCTOBER

19 Anthony Browne, 1st
Viscount Montagu, died
(1592)

20 Henri, Duke of Anjou, was
suggested as a suitor for
Elizabeth (1570)

21 Elizabeth stayed with
Earl of Arundel at
Nonsuch Palace (1574)

22 Henry Parker, 11th Baron
Morley, died in exile (1577)

23 Charles Howard was
created Earl of Nottingham
(1597)

24 Edward Stanley, 3rd
Earl of Derby and Privy
Councillor, died (1572)

25 John Somerville travelled to London, planning to assassinate Elizabeth (1583)

26 Mildred Cooke, Lady Cecil, wrote that she had taken Mary, daughter of Sir Henry Sidney, into her household (1570)

27 Elizabeth wrote to her half-sister, Mary, apologising for a delay caused to one of Mary's servants (1552)

28 **Feast of SS Simon and Jude, Apostles**

Thomas Causton, composer, died (1570)

29 Lord Mayor of London's Procession (1568)

30 Elizabeth refused to renew Earl of Essex's monopoly on import of sweet wines (1485)

31 All Hallows' Eve

Sir Nicholas Hare, Speaker
of the House of Commons,
died (1557)

Notes

Notes

MONTH PLANNER

November

1 William Brooke, 10th Baron Cobham, was born (1572)

2 Gilbert Berkeley, Bishop of Bath and Wells, died (1581)

3 Sir John Perrot, Privy Councillor, died in Tower of London (1592)

4 Marie of Guise, Regent of Scotland, processed through London to dine with Edward VI (1551)

5 Elizabeth rebuked Lords and Commons for their petition for her to marry and to name an heir (1566)

6 Mary I acknowledged Elizabeth as her heir (1558)

7 Henri II of France entered Calais (1558)

8 Thanksgiving at court for victory at the Battle of Lepanto (1571)

9 Commons ordered members who left without the Speaker's licence to pay fourpence into the poor box (1566)

10 Robert Devereux, 2nd Earl of Essex, was born (1565)

11 Richard Madox, diarist and clergyman, was born (1546)

12 Parliamentary deputation urged Elizabeth to consent to Mary, Queen of Scots' execution (1586)

13 Edward Squire was hanged, drawn and quartered for attempting to poison Elizabeth and Essex (1597)

14 Lord Burghley moved in Parliament that absent lords who had not sent proxies should be admonished (1594)

15 Robert Bowes, MP and ambassador, died (1597)

16 Charles Neville, 6th Earl of Westmorland, died in Flanders (1601)

17 Mary I of England died and Elizabeth ascended the throne (1558)

18 First informal meeting of Elizabeth's Privy Council held at Hatfield Palace (1558)

19 Robert Dudley appointed as Master of the Horse (1558)

20 Sir Christopher Hatton, Lord Chancellor, died (1590)

21 Sir Thomas Gresham, merchant, founder of Royal Exchange and Gresham College, died (1579)

22 Elizabeth left Hatfield and rode towards London (1558)

23 Elizabeth stayed at the Charterhouse, on outskirts of London, prior to entering the city as queen (1558)

24 Sir William Cecil was sent to Tower of London following downfall of Duke of Somerset (1549)

25 Cecil learnt Elizabeth's relationship with Robert Dudley was gossip of the French Court (1560)

26 Elizabeth attended an archery match in St James' Park (1561)

27 Lady Katherine Grey secretly married Edward Seymour, Earl of Hertford (1560)

28 Elizabeth made her first ceremonial entry into London as queen, staying at Tower of London (1558)

29 Douglass Howard, Lady Sheffield, married Sir Edward Stafford (1579)

30 Elizabeth made her famous 'Golden Speech' to House of Commons (1601)

Birthdays	Anniversaries	Reminders	Projects

Gardening	Events	Occasions	Festivals

Elizabeth's Accession

The 1544 Act of Succession had provided for Elizabeth to inherit the throne if neither of her elder half-siblings had children of their own. By the summer of 1558, it was clear that her half-sister, Queen Mary, was in failing health and would never bear a child. The early autumn saw a procession of courtiers waiting upon Elizabeth at Hatfield. This was a depressing lesson in the speedy transfer of loyalty from a reigning monarch to a future one that Elizabeth learnt from to such an extent that she refused to name a successor. Mary herself had put off accepting the inevitable, but by 6 November she could no longer avoid the knowledge that she was dying. Two of her servants were sent to Elizabeth to inform her that the queen recognised her as her successor, and hoped that she would maintain the Catholic faith. Influenza was sweeping the country, and it was probably that which finally carried Mary off in the early hours of 17th November. Immediately, her coronation ring was taken from her finger and carried to Hatfield as fast as a man could gallop. Elizabeth took it, then, sinking to her knees, cried out a verse from Psalm 118: 'This is the Lord's doing, and it is marvellous in our eyes'. Meanwhile, in London, she had been proclaimed queen at Westminster and at St Paul's

Cross. She was probably equally pleased to hear of the death the following day of Reginald Pole, the Archbishop of Canterbury. Not only had he reconciled England to Rome, but he was also one of the last men to carry the blood of the house of York. His demise would enable her to choose an archbishop whose views were closer to her own. She was already considering what her religious route should be. She was inclined to Protestantism, but was not so radical as her half-brother, Edward VI, had been.

Elizabeth remained at Hatfield for a few days. Her first appointments were to the two men who were to remain her closest advisers until they died – Lord Robert Dudley was appointed her Master of the Horse, and Sir William Cecil took the role of Secretary. On 23rd November, Elizabeth arrived at the Charterhouse, home of Lord North, where she remained until she proceeded to the Tower of London on 28th November.

HATFIELD PALACE

Elizabeth had a long association with Hatfield Palace, from its earliest days as one of her nursery houses. Her country residence prior to becoming queen, it was the place to which she retreated during difficult times in the reigns of Edward VI and Mary I.

Owned by the Bishops of Ely, Hatfield Palace was located some 20 miles north of London on the Great North Road. Around 1480, Bishop John Morton built a new red-brick palace, comprising four ranges around a central courtyard, sited to the east of the Bishops' medieval manor house.

Henry VIII visited regularly, staying for several weeks in 1522 whilst avoiding the plague in London, and again in 1528 to avoid a severe epidemic of the sweating sickness. His sister, Mary, the French Queen, was staying at Hatfield in 1516 when she gave birth to her daughter, Frances Brandon (mother of Lady Jane Grey), who was baptised at the adjacent St Etheldreda's church.

Elizabeth was first taken to Hatfield as a baby in December 1533. Her older half-sister Mary was sent to reside in her younger sister's household there for a time too. In 1538, Henry VIII acquired Hatfield Palace and continued to use it primarily as a nursery.

Granted Hatfield after her father's death, Elizabeth spent lengthy periods there during the reigns of her siblings. It was there, in 1549, that she was interrogated by Sir Robert Tyrwhitt for two weeks, over her relationship with Sir Thomas Seymour. Elizabeth was also at Hatfield when Edward died, a suitable distance from the dramatic events of 1553, which saw Lady Jane Grey briefly on the throne before Mary successfully claimed it. She was there again in November 1558 when Mary died and she learned of her own accession to the throne.

During her reign, Elizabeth visited Hatfield occasionally on her summer progresses; her longest stays, lasting a week or so, were in 1568 and 1571.

Following Elizabeth's death, James VI & I exchanged Hatfield Palace for the Cecils' house and estate at Theobalds. In 1607–12, Robert Cecil built a grand new house at Hatfield, close to the Tudor palace. This Jacobean Hatfield House remains in the Cecil family to this day and is open to visitors. All that remains of Hatfield Palace are the gatehouse and west range, containing the Great Hall, and they can be viewed as part of a visit to Hatfield House.

NOVEMBER

1   **All Hallows' Day**

William Brooke, 10th
Baron Cobham, was born
(1572)

2   Gilbert Berkeley, Bishop of
Bath and Wells, died (1581)

3   Sir John Perrot, Privy
Councillor, died in Tower
of London (1592)

4   Marie of Guise, Regent
      of Scotland, processed
      through London to dine
      with Edward VI (1551)

5   Elizabeth rebuked Lords
      and Commons for their
      petition for her to marry
      and to name an heir (1566)

6   Mary I acknowledged
      Elizabeth as her heir (1558)

NOVEMBER

7   Henri II of France entered
Calais (1558)

8   Thanksgiving at court for
victory at the Battle of
Lepanto (1571)

9   Commons ordered members
who left without the
Speaker's licence to pay
fourpence into the poor box
(1566)

10 Robert Devereux, 2nd Earl of Essex, was born (1565)

11 Richard Madox, diarist and clergyman, was born (1546)

12 Parliamentary deputation urged Elizabeth to consent to Mary, Queen of Scots' execution (1586)

NOVEMBER

13 Edward Squire was hanged,
drawn and quartered
for attempting to poison
Elizabeth and Essex (1597)

_____

_____

_____

_____

_____

_____

_____

_____

14 Lord Burghley moved in
Parliament that absent lords
who had not sent proxies
should be admonished
(1594)

_____

_____

_____

_____

_____

_____

_____

15 Robert Bowes, MP and
ambassador, died (1597)

_____

_____

_____

_____

_____

_____

_____

_____

16 Charles Neville, 6th Earl
of Westmorland, died in
Flanders (1601)

17 Mary I of England died
and Elizabeth ascended the
throne (1558)

18 First informal meeting of
Elizabeth's Privy Council
held at Hatfield Palace
(1558)

NOVEMBER

19 Robert Dudley appointed as Master of the Horse (1558)

20 Sir Christopher Hatton, Lord Chancellor, died (1590)

21 Sir Thomas Gresham, merchant, founder of Royal Exchange and Gresham College, died (1579)

22 Elizabeth left Hatfield
and rode towards London
(1558)

_____
_____
_____
_____
_____
_____
_____
_____

23 Elizabeth stayed at the
Charterhouse, on outskirts
of London, prior to
entering the city as queen
(1558)

_____
_____
_____
_____
_____
_____
_____

24 Sir William Cecil was
sent to Tower of London
following downfall of Duke
of Somerset (1549)

_____
_____
_____
_____
_____
_____
_____

NOVEMBER

25 Cecil learnt Elizabeth's relationship with Robert Dudley was gossip of the French Court (1560)

26 Elizabeth attended an archery match in St James' Park (1561)

27 Lady Katherine Grey secretly married Edward Seymour, Earl of Hertford (1560)

November

28 Elizabeth made her first
ceremonial entry into
London as queen, staying at
Tower of London (1558)

29 Douglass Howard, Lady
Sheffield, married Sir
Edward Stafford (1579)

30 **St Andrew the Apostle's
Day**

Elizabeth made her famous
'Golden Speech' to House
of Commons (1601)

NOVEMBER

Notes

Notes

MONTH PLANNER
December

1 Elizabeth gave audience to Spanish ambassador, de Silva, at Whitehall (1566)

2 Edward Wright, mathematician and cartographer, buried (1615)

3 Elizabeth wrote to Mountjoy, Lord Lieutenant of Ireland, assuring him of her goodwill (1600)

4 Mary, Queen of Scots was publicly declared guilty of treason against Elizabeth (1586)

5 François II, King of France and King of Scots, died (1560)

6 Elizabeth was guest of Sir Robert Cecil at the Savoy, London (1602)

7 Elizabeth's godson, son of Sir William Brooke, 10th Baron Cobham, was christened at court (1560)

8 Mary, Queen of Scots was born (1542)

9 Earl of Leicester sailed to the Netherlands to command English forces there (1585)

10 John, Lord Sheffield died, freeing his wife, Douglass Howard, to become Leicester's mistress (1568)

11 Elizabeth stayed at Arundel House, London, as guest of Earl of Nottingham (1602)

12 Anne of Denmark, Queen of Scots, was born (1574)

13 Francis Drake left Plymouth on trip in which he circumnavigated world (1577)

14 Mary I was buried at Westminster Abbey (1558)

15 Spanish ambassador, Guerau de Espes, expelled from England for his role in Ridolfi Plot (1571)

16 Earl of Oxford, Lord Dudley and Lord Herbert each wed at Court (1571)

17 Matthew Parker was consecrated as Archbishop of Canterbury (1559)

18 Thomas Sackville, Baron Buckhurst, was installed as Knight of the Garter (1589)

19 Elizabeth attended wedding of Anne Cecil and Earl of Oxford (1571)

20 Sir Francis Walsingham was appointed second Principal Secretary (1573)

21 Sir John Shelton, Controller of the Household of Elizabeth and Mary, died (1539)

22 Elizabeth was guest of Sir Robert Cecil at the Strand, London (1600)

23 Elizabeth moved from Somerset House to Whitehall Palace, which became her principal residence (1558)

24 The English defeated the Irish at Battle of Kinsale (1601)

25 Lettice Knollys, Countess of Leicester, died (1634)

26 Elizabeth wrote to Earl of Warwick of her relief at the collapse of the Rising of the North (1568)

27 Katherine Cooke, Lady Killigrew, died (1583)

28 Sir Nicholas Bacon, Lord Keeper of the Great Seal, was born (1510)

29 George Clifford, 3rd Earl of Cumberland, was buried (1605)

30 Roger Ascham, Elizabeth's tutor, died (1568)

31 Elizabeth chartered the East India Company (1600)

Birthdays	Anniversaries	Reminders	Projects

Gardening	Events	Occasions	Festivals

THE RISING OF THE NORTH

When Elizabeth ascended the throne, she implemented a religious settlement that was perhaps more Protestant than she first intended. The further away from London, the more Catholic the population tended to be, and the great nobles of the north, the earls of Northumberland and Westmorland, clung to the old faith, as well as to dreams of the power of their feudal ancestors.

When Mary, Queen of Scots arrived as an exile in England, the Earl of Northumberland suggested that a marriage between her and Philip of Spain might be a way to turn England back to Rome, but Philip did not think this feasible.

The following year, the Earl of Westmorland's brother-in-law, the Duke of Norfolk, who was a Protestant, but unhappy at Elizabeth's reliance on Sir William Cecil, suggested a marriage between himself and the Scottish queen. Mary would, he thought, convert to Protestantism, and the two would rule England after Elizabeth's death. Westmorland and Northumberland were persuaded of the merits of the plan by Mary. Norfolk also had support amongst his fellow councillors, including from the Earl of Leicester, but he lacked the courage to ask Elizabeth's consent. She soon found out what was being mooted, but it became a test of Norfolk's loyalty for him to inform her. He failed to do so and withdrew from court. The Northern earls wrote that they would support him in rebellion, and, at first, he contemplated the idea before having a change of heart and setting out to confess all to the queen. Before he could enter her presence, he was arrested and sent to the Tower. Smarting from the betrayal, Elizabeth summoned Westmorland and Northumberland. Fearing that they would likewise be imprisoned, the earls gave the signal for rebellion. On 14th November, accompanied by 300 armed men, they entered Durham Cathedral, where a Catholic Mass was offered. Two days later, they headed south. Wherever they passed, the churches were packed with people eager to worship in the old way, but the earls could not command the support of their fellow magnates or the northern gentry, and an army of untrained countrymen was of little use.

Lacking money and a coherent objective, the earls retreated, fleeing to Scotland while the Countess of Westmorland escaped to Flanders. Northumberland was handed over by the Scots and executed at York. Elizabeth was eager to set an example and over 500 men were hanged.

PALACE OF WHITEHALL

The Palace of Whitehall was once the largest in Europe, with over 1,500 rooms that roughly covered the area today from Big Ben to Trafalgar Square; but, sadly, now only vestiges remain. Following the downfall of Cardinal Wolsey in 1529, Henry VIII appropriated York Place, the London residence of the archbishops of York. He and Anne Boleyn worked on the designs for expanding York Place, where they planned to spend time together away from Henry's first wife, Katharine of Aragon.

The palace's unusual design straddled the public thoroughfare, now known as Whitehall, with the royal privy apartments added to Wolsey's Great Hall and chapel on the east side of the street, beside the River Thames. Extensive recreation facilities, including a large tiltyard, tennis courts, cockpit and bowling alleys, were located on the west side of the street, with large hunting parks beyond; recognised today as St James's, Green, Hyde and Regent's Parks.

The two sides of the palace were connected by the Holbein Gate to the north and King St Gate to the south, enabling Henry and his nobles to move from one side to the other without crossing the public road. It is within a room in the Holbein Gate that Henry VIII secretly married Anne Boleyn in January 1533, and later that year the palace was also the location of celebrations for Anne's coronation.

Whitehall became Henry VIII's principal official residence from 1532, although parts of it remained a building site throughout his reign. The palace was also Elizabeth's primary official residence during her 44-year reign and the one at which she spent most time. It was Elizabeth who finally completed the building of Whitehall, finishing the work begun by her father and mother 25 years beforehand.

Whitehall provided a magnificent setting for meetings with ambassadors and dignitaries from European courts and it was used frequently during Elizabeth's marriage negotiations to display the queen's splendour, along with her power and wealth. Following her death at Richmond Palace, Elizabeth's body was brought to Whitehall Palace where she lay in state, kept watch over by her ladies, prior to her funeral and burial at Westminster Abbey.

In 1691 a fire ruined much of the palace and a subsequent fire in 1698 destroyed it. Some remnants of the Tudor palace can be found around Whitehall; Cardinal Wolsey's wine cellar lies under the Ministry of Defence building and fragments of Henry VIII's tennis courts are within the building now occupied by the Cabinet Office.

DECEMBER

1 Elizabeth gave audience to Spanish ambassador, de Silva, at Whitehall (1566)

_____
_____
_____
_____
_____
_____
_____
_____

2 Edward Wright, mathematician and cartographer, buried (1615)

_____
_____
_____
_____
_____
_____
_____

3 Elizabeth wrote to Mountjoy, Lord Lieutenant of Ireland, assuring him of her goodwill (1600)

_____
_____
_____
_____
_____
_____
_____

4   Mary, Queen of Scots was
    publicly declared guilty of
    treason against Elizabeth
    (1586)

5   François II, King of France
    and King of Scots, died
    (1560)

6   Elizabeth was guest of Sir
    Robert Cecil at the Savoy,
    London (1602)

DECEMBER

7 Elizabeth's godson, son
of Sir William Brooke,
10th Baron Cobham, was
christened at court (1560)

8 Mary, Queen of Scots was
born (1542)

9 Earl of Leicester sailed
to the Netherlands to
command English forces
there (1585)

10 John, Lord Sheffield died, freeing his wife, Douglass Howard, to become Leicester's mistress (1568)

11 Elizabeth stayed at Arundel House, London, as guest of the Earl of Nottingham (1602)

12 Anne of Denmark, Queen of Scots, was born (1574)

December

13   Francis Drake left Plymouth
on a trip in which he
circumnavigated the world
(1577)

14   Mary I was buried at
Westminster Abbey (1558)

15   Spanish ambassador,
Guerau de Espes, expelled
from England for his role in
Ridolfi Plot (1571)

16 Earl of Oxford, Lord Dudley and Lord Herbert each wed at Court (1571)

17 Matthew Parker was consecrated as Archbishop of Canterbury (1559)

18 Thomas Sackville, Baron Buckhurst, was installed as a Knight of the Garter (1589)

DECEMBER

19 Elizabeth attended wedding of Anne Cecil and Earl of Oxford (1571)

_____
_____
_____
_____
_____
_____
_____
_____
_____

20 Sir Francis Walsingham was appointed second Principal Secretary (1573)

_____
_____
_____
_____
_____
_____
_____
_____
_____

21 **St Thomas the Apostle's Day**

Sir John Shelton, Controller of the Household of Elizabeth and Mary, died (1539)

_____
_____
_____
_____
_____
_____
_____
_____

22 Elizabeth was guest of Sir Robert Cecil at the Strand, London (1600)

_____

_____

_____

_____

_____

_____

_____

_____

23 Elizabeth moved from Somerset House to Whitehall Palace, which became her principal residence (1558)

_____

_____

_____

_____

_____

_____

_____

24 The English defeated the Irish at Battle of Kinsale (1601)

_____

_____

_____

_____

_____

_____

_____

December

25 **Nativity of Christ (Christmas)**

Lettice Knollys, Countess of Leicester, died (1634)

26 **St Stephen's Day**

Elizabeth wrote to Earl of Warwick of her relief at the collapse of the Rising of the North (1568)

27 **St John the Apostle's Day**

Katherine Cooke, Lady Killigrew, died (1583)

28 **Feast of the Holy Innocents**

Sir Nicholas Bacon, Lord Keeper of the Great Seal, was born (1510)

29 George Clifford, 3rd Earl of Cumberland, was buried (1605)

30 Roger Ascham, Elizabeth's tutor, died (1568)

December

31   Elizabeth chartered the
East India Company (1600)

Notes

Notes

INDEX OF PEOPLE

Many people of the period did not use surnames, so are listed under their first name. Women are listed under their maiden names, as many married more than once. If their married name is well known, it is added in brackets.

Anne of Cleves, Queen of England (1515–1557) Daughter of Duke John of Cleves and Duchess Maria of Jülich-Berg, Anne was chosen to marry Henry VIII to cement an anti-Imperial alliance. Delighted with her portrait, Henry looked forward to the marriage, but found Anne unattractive in the flesh. An amicable annulment was arranged, and Anne remained in England, on good terms with Henry and his children.

Ascham, Roger (1515–1568) Ascham studied at St John's College, Cambridge, and lectured there in Greek. He was appointed Latin and Greek tutor to the Lady Elizabeth, despite opposition from her step-mother, Katherine Parr. Ascham was appointed Latin secretary to Mary I, then Elizabeth I. His most famous work was a treatise on archery, and another on Latin pedagogy entitled *The Schoolmaster*.

Astley (or Ashley), Sir John (c. 1507–1596) A distant connection of the queen's through the Boleyn family, he was the husband of Katherine Champernowne, Elizabeth I's Governess, and First Lady of the Bedchamber. During the early part of Elizabeth's reign, he was a member of the inner court circle but after Katherine's death lived a more retired life. He served on many Parliamentary committees, and Commissions.

Astley (or Ashley), Katherine, née Champernowne (c. 1502–1565) Katherine was Elizabeth's governess. An early convert to religious reform, along with her sister, Lady Denny, who was a friend of Katherine Parr's, her influence was formative for Elizabeth. She spent a short period in the Tower after failing to protect Elizabeth from the advances of Sir Thomas Seymour. Elizabeth remained devoted to her, appointing her as First Lady of the Bedchamber on her accession.

Bacon, Sir Nicholas (1510–1579) A courtier and politician, Sir Nicholas was a graduate of Corpus Christi College, Cambridge and Lord Keeper of the Great Seal.

Berkeley, Gilbert, Bishop of Bath and Wells (d. 1581) Initially a member of the Franciscan Order, Berkeley's views had become so Protestant by 1554 that he left England for the Calvinist community at Frankfurt. He returned on Elizabeth's succession, became a royal chaplain, and bishop of Bath and Wells in 1560. His episcopacy was plagued with financial worries and arguments over the Vestiarian Controversy. He made a secret marriage to a woman of humble birth.

Boleyn, Anne, Queen of England (c. 1501–1536) Daughter of Sir Thomas Boleyn, a diplomat at Henry VIII's court, and Lady Elizabeth Howard, sister of the Duke of Norfolk, Anne's long love affair with Henry VIII changed the course of English history. Unable to procure an annulment of his first marriage to Katharine of Aragon, Henry eventually threw off papal authority and the couple married secretly in January 1533, when Anne was a few weeks pregnant with a daughter, who would become Elizabeth I. Anne was executed on, almost certainly false, charges of adultery, incest and treason, three years after she married Henry.

Boleyn, Sir Thomas, Earl of Wiltshire and Ormond (c 1477–1539) Boleyn, an ambassador for Henry VIII, was the father of Mary, Anne and George Boleyn and thus briefly father-in-law to Henry VIII, and grandfather to Elizabeth I.

Brooke, William, 10th Baron Cobham (1527–1597) After spending some of his youth in Venice, he joined first the Boulogne then the Calais garrisons and served on several embassies to France. Northumberland appointed him to the Privy Council in 1550. In December 1558 Elizabeth gave him a special embassy to announce the death of Mary to Philip of Spain. He was appointed Lord Warden of the Cinque Ports and was a close political ally of Sir William Cecil. His second wife was one of Elizabeth's ladies.

Byrd, William (c. 1540–1623) Following an early career as organist and choirmaster at Lincoln Cathedral, Byrd returned to his native London in 1568. He became a member of the Chapel Royal, where he worked closely with Thomas Tallis. The two shared a monopoly for the publication of printed music in England and Elizabeth ignored Byrd's frequent citations for recusancy.

Catherine de' Medici, Queen of France (1519–1589) Catherine, niece of Pope Clement VII, was unhappily married to Henri II at the age of 14. On his death in 1559 she vied with the Guise family for influence in the reign of her son François II. On his death she assumed the regency for first Charles IX, then Henri III. Despite her efforts to mediate the Wars of Religion, her actions contributed significantly to the Massacre of Bartholomew's Day.

Carey, Sir Henry, 1st Baron Hunsdon (1526–1596) Son of William Carey and Mary Boleyn, Hunsdon was a favourite of his first cousin, Elizabeth I, holding senior positions at her court. He was a Knight of the Garter and a Privy Councillor. Carey was also patron of William Shakespeare's playing company, the Lord Chamberlain's Men.

Carey, Katherine, Lady Knollys (1524–1569) Katherine was Elizabeth's maternal first cousin and one of the queen's closest friends. Lady Knollys and her husband, Sir Francis, were Protestants, who went into exile during Mary's reign. On their return, Katherine and two of her daughters were appointed to Elizabeth's household. Lady Knollys bore fourteen children in all. Elizabeth was devastated at her death.

Carey, Katherine, Countess of Nottingham (1547–1603) Daughter of Elizabeth I's cousin, Henry Carey, 1st Baron Hunsdon, Katherine married Charles Howard, later 2nd Baron Howard of Effingham, Lord High Admiral of England and 1st Earl of Nottingham. They had five children. Katherine served Elizabeth for 45 years and her death on 25th February 1603 was a great blow to Elizabeth, who died a month later.

Cavendish, Elizabeth (1555–1582) Daughter of Sir William Cavendish and Bess of Hardwick, one of the wealthiest women of the Tudor period, Elizabeth married Charles Stuart, 1st Earl of Lennox, younger brother of Henry Stuart, Lord Darnley, without the necessary royal permission, incurring Elizabeth I's wrath.

Cecil, Anne, Countess of Oxford (1556–1588) The daughter of William Cecil and his second wife, Mildred Cooke, Anne benefited from the academic education that elite women received in the mid-sixteenth century. She was betrothed to Philip Sidney, but married her father's ward, the Earl of Oxford. The couple were unhappy – he accused her, with no apparent justification, of adultery and refused to recognise their daughter. They were formally reconciled and had three further children.

Cecil, William, 1st Baron Burghley (1520–1598) William Cecil first came to prominence in the reign of Edward VI as Secretary to Lord Protector Somerset, then to the Privy Council as a whole. He was Surveyor of Elizabeth's lands, enabling them to maintain contact during Mary's reign. On Elizabeth's accession, he was appointed Secretary, and remained her most important and influential councillor until his death. Elizabeth was attached to him personally, as well as politically.

Cecil, Sir Robert, (1563–1612) He succeeded his father, William, as Elizabeth's chief minister, to the disgust of the Earl of Essex, but never had the personal rapport with her that William had had. He worked tirelessly to ensure the succession of the Protestant James VI of Scotland, and retained his offices and lands after Elizabeth's death.

Chatillon, Odet de Coligny, Cardinal de, (1517–1571) A peer of France and a member of the Royal Council under Henri II, by 1561 he had become a Huguenot. Summoned to appear in Rome, he refused to attend, and was initially protected by Charles IX. He worked with Catherine de' Medici to conciliate the Wars of Religion, but failed. In 1568 he sought and was granted asylum in England, along with his wife, Isabelle de Hauteville. He continued his efforts to affect reconciliation, promoting a marriage between Elizabeth and the Duke of Anjou, but died at Canterbury en route to France.

Clifford, George, 3rd Earl of Cumberland (1558–1605) Although a Catholic, Cumberland's father had avoided involvement in the Rising of the North, and George, on inheriting in 1570, became a ward of the Protestant Earl of Bedford, whose daughter he married. He was a keen mathematician and a devoted courtier, becoming Queen's Champion in 1590. He had a sideline as a privateer.

Clinton, Edward Fiennes de, 1st Earl of Lincoln (1512–1585) Clinton was the second husband of Henry VIII's mistress, Elizabeth Blount. He was favoured by the king and served in the Pilgrimage of Grace and as Lord High Admiral in the Wars of the Rough Wooing against Scotland. He was imprisoned for holding the Tower against Mary, but later pardoned and reappointed as Admiral during the war with France. He was Privy Councillor to Elizabeth, and his third wife, Elizabeth FitzGerald, was one of her closest friends.

Dee, John (1527–c. 1609) A graduate of St John's College, Cambridge, Dee mixed the study of mathematics with astrology, alchemy and navigation in true Renaissance style and amassed a large library. He advised Elizabeth on the most auspicious date for her coronation and other astrological matters.

Douglas, Margaret, Countess of Lennox (1515–1578) Elizabeth's first cousin, the two had an uneasy relationship. Lady Lennox had been a close friend of Mary I, who had considered promoting her above Elizabeth in the succession. She intrigued tirelessly for her son, Lord Darnley, to marry her niece, Mary, Queen of Scots.

Devereux, Robert, 2nd Earl of Essex (1565–1601) Son of Walter Devereux and Lettice Knollys, Essex became the step-son of Elizabeth I's favourite, Robert Dudley, Earl of Leicester, when his mother re-married. Essex married Frances Walsingham, the daughter of Elizabeth I's spymaster, Sir Francis Walsingham, and they had five children. Highly favoured by the queen following the death of Leicester, Essex, although brilliant and courageous, was also proud and quarrelsome. As Elizabeth aged, her court became riven by factions, largely led by Essex in opposition to the queen's new chief minister, Robert Cecil. Matters came to a head when Essex led an ill-fated rebellion against the queen and was executed for treason.

Devereux, Walter, 1st Earl of Essex (1541–1576) A distant cousin of the queen's and an ardent Protestant, he served her faithfully, commanding forces against the Rising of the North. He married Lettice Knollys, another of Elizabeth's relatives, and was appointed Lord Deputy of Ireland. Like many others, he found this an impossible task, although he attempted to carry it out with considerable brutality, massacring the followers of O'Neill.

Drake, Sir Francis (c. 1540–1596) A sailor, explorer and privateer, Drake's daring exploits against Spanish shipping and naval towns, including the great port of Cadiz, made him famous. He circumnavigated the world in the *Pelican* 1577–1580. Drake was second-in-command of the English fleet against the Spanish Armada of 1588.

Dudley, Ambrose, Earl of Warwick (c. 1530–1590)
Son of the Duke of Northumberland, Ambrose spent a period in prison in 1553–4, but was released and served in Philip's army in France. In 1561, Elizabeth permitted him to inherit the family titles of Baron Lisle and Earl of Warwick, and he led her forces at Newhaven with distinction. He raised forces to march against the Rising of the North, but withdrew when it collapsed. He became a Privy Councillor in 1573. He remained his brother, Leicester's, closest friend and supporter, but was also loved by the queen for himself.

Dudley, John, Duke of Northumberland (c. 1504–1553)
Dudley was recognised by Henry VIII as a competent general and excellent admiral and he appointed him as a councillor for the regency of Edward VI. By late 1549, he dominated both king and council and took the title of Duke of Northumberland. In May 1553, he arranged the marriage of his son, Guildford, to Lady Jane Grey, whom the king, shortly after, nominated to succeed him in an attempt to overturn the Act of Succession. Whatever his original level of involvement in the plan, Northumberland took it up with enthusiasm, but it did not succeed and he was executed, having made a last-minute confession of his return to the Catholic faith.

Dudley, Robert, Earl of Leicester (c. 1533–1588)
The fifth son of the Duke of Northumberland, Robert was well educated by Protestant tutors and became a companion to the young Edward, Prince of Wales. He married Amy Robsart, daughter of a Norfolk gentleman, apparently for love. Robert was imprisoned following the attempt to enthrone his sister-in-law, Lady Jane Grey, but Queen Mary released him to serve in King Philip's army. On Elizabeth's accession, Robert became Master of the Horse. Elizabeth seemed deeply in love with him, and Amy's mysterious death was rumoured to be murder. Elizabeth favoured him for the rest of his life, granting him the title of Earl of Leicester and making him a Privy Councillor.

Edward VI, King of England (1537–1553)
The longed-for male heir of Henry VIII and his third wife, Jane Seymour, Edward became king at the age of nine. He was an ardent Protestant and attempted to bequeath the crown to his equally Protestant cousin, Lady Jane Grey, ahead of his half-sisters, Mary and Elizabeth. His short reign ended with his early death, aged 15.

Elizabeth of York (1466–1503)
Elizabeth's grandmother, she was the eldest daughter of Edward IV and Elizabeth Woodville, the death of her father turned her world upside down. Her uncle, Richard of Gloucester, pronounced Elizabeth and her siblings illegitimate and seized the throne. The Lancastrian claimant, Henry, Earl of Richmond, swore to marry her if he became king. Following his coronation as Henry VII, they were married and lived together harmoniously for 17 years, before Elizabeth's death in childbirth.

FitzAlan, Henry, 12th Earl of Arundel (1512–1580)
His career began well under Henry VIII, as Deputy of Calais, and Privy Councillor. Under Edward, he clashed with both Somerset and Northumberland, and was sent to the Tower. Arundel, along with Pembroke, was the first to break ranks against the attempt to enthrone Lady Jane Grey. He was Mary's President of the Council, and gave her away at her wedding to Philip. While he was opposed to Elizabeth's imprisonment in 1554, and became one of her Privy Councillors, he did not achieve great success in her reign.

François, Duke of Anjou (1555–1584)
A younger son of King Henri II of France, François led a moderate group, the Politiques, in the Wars of Religion, and attempted to become the leader of the opposition to Spain's control of the Netherlands. He was the most serious formal suitor for Elizabeth's hand.

François II, King of France (1544–1560)
François inherited the French throne at the age of 15. Married to Mary, Queen of Scots, his short reign was dominated by her Guise relatives. He died painfully of an abscess in the ear.

Gresham, Sir Thomas (c. 1519–1579)
Gresham, son of a lord mayor, came from a well-established London merchant family. His financial acumen brought him favour from all the Tudor monarchs in whose reigns he lived. His years of experience in Antwerp led him to propose the founding of a 'bourse' in London, and he funded the development of the Royal Exchange in 1565.

Grey, Lady Katherine (c. 1540–1568)
Katherine was Elizabeth's heir under the will of Henry VIII, although her claim was disputed. Her secret marriage to the Earl of Hertford infuriated the queen, and the couple was sent to the Tower of London. Katherine was eventually released to house arrest, but died after several years of miserable existence, parted from her husband and children.

Hardwick, Elizabeth (Bess), Countess of Shrewsbury (c. 1527–1608) Bess' four marriages raised her from minor gentry to the richest woman in England, after the queen. Her fourth marriage foundered under the strain of keeping the Queen of Scots prisoner, but she gained consolation from her building projects at Chatsworth and Hardwick and her hopes that her granddaughter, Lady Arbella Stuart, might succeed the queen. In this she was disappointed.

Hastings, Henry, 3rd Earl of Huntingdon (c. 1536–1595) Known as the 'Puritan earl', he was a descendant of the house of York and occasionally talked of as a successor to Elizabeth. Wisely, he shunned such ideas and was her devoted servant. After the failure of the Rising of the North, he was appointed as Lord President of the Council of the North.

Hatton, Sir Christopher (c. 1540–1591)
Hatton was not of exalted birth, but around 1564 he caught the queen's eye and was appointed as a Gentleman Pensioner. Soon, he was talked of as rivalling the Earl of Leicester in Elizabeth's affections. She gave him a nickname – her 'Lids', complimenting Leicester as her 'Eyes'. He became Lord Chancellor in 1587.

Henri IV, King of France (1553–1610) The Huguenot King of Navarre, he inherited the crown of France from his brother-in-law and distant cousin, King Henri III. Formerly an ally of Elizabeth's, to end the Wars of Religion he converted to Catholicism and ruled successfully until he was assassinated.

Henry VII, King of England (1457–1509)
Descended through his grandmother, Katherine de Valois, from the French kings, and through his mother, Lady Margaret Beaufort, from Edward III, most of Henry's youth was spent in exile, as the last remnant of the house of Lancaster. He led a successful invasion of England in 1485 and, winning the crown in battle, became the first monarch of the Tudor dynasty.

Henry VIII, King of England (1491–1547)
The second son of Henry VII and Elizabeth of York, Henry began his reign in traditional fashion, promoting war with France and expressing strong support for papal authority. By the late 1520s, however, a combination of dynastic fears and his passion for Anne Boleyn led him to request Pope Clement VII to grant an annulment of his marriage to Katharine of Aragon. When it was not forthcoming, he broke with Rome, took the title Supreme Head of the Church in England and pursued a policy of ruthless repression of all dissent. Henry married a total of six times, but still left a minor heir, a disputed succession, and a country that was almost bankrupt despite the huge injection of cash from the Dissolution of the Monasteries.

Heneage, Michael (1540–1600) Brother of one of Elizabeth's Gentlemen of the Privy Chamber, Heneage sat in four of her Parliaments. He assisted Robert Hare in the compilation of Cambridge's archives and records, and Thomas Milles in his creation of the Catalogue of Honour. He delivered papers to the Elizabethan society of antiquaries, and some of his papers are in the Cotton Collection at the British Library.

Herbert, William, 1st Earl of Pembroke (c. 1506–1570) Herbert entered the service of the king's cousin, the Earl of Worcester, then became one of Henry VIII's Gentlemen Pensioners. His career blossomed when his wife's sister, Katherine Parr, became Henry's sixth wife. Prominent in the government of Edward VI, he stamped out the Prayer Book Rebellion of 1549, along with Bedford. Close to Northumberland, he abandoned him when the tide turned towards Mary in 1553 and fought successfully in the English campaign in France in 1557. He was one of the first men appointed to Elizabeth's Privy Council and served until his death.

Howard, Douglass, Lady Sheffield (1543–1608) Douglass and her sister, Frances, were both rumoured to be in love with the queen's favourite, Lord Robert Dudley, but in 1560 Douglass left court to marry Lord Sheffield. She was widowed with two children in 1568 and began an affair with Dudley, now Earl of Leicester. He refused to marry her for fear of Elizabeth's wrath and the affair ended after the birth of a son. She later claimed they had been married but could not prove the case. He was rumoured to have poisoned her husband, but that is extremely unlikely.

Howard, Katheryn, Queen of England (c. 1521–1542) The fifth wife of Henry VIII, Katheryn was no more than 20 when she married the 49-year-old King. The daughter of Lord Edmund Howard, a younger son of Thomas Howard, 2nd Duke of Norfolk, and Joyce Culpeper, she was a first cousin of Anne Boleyn. Katheryn was executed for alleged adultery within two years of her marriage.

Howard, Philip, 13th Earl of Arundel (1557–1595) The son of the 4th Duke of Norfolk, Philip hoped to escape the taint of treason after Norfolk's execution by spending lavishly to win Elizabeth's favour, but she did not take to him. He inherited the ancient earldom of Arundel through his mother and married Anne Dacre, who converted to Catholicism. He too began to waver in his Protestantism, and was received into the Catholic Church in 1584. He was captured attempting to leave the country and spent the rest of his life in the Tower. He was later canonised by the Roman Catholic Church.

Howard, Thomas, 4th Duke of Norfolk (1536–1572) Son of Henry Howard, Earl of Surrey, Thomas inherited the dukedom of Norfolk from his grandfather.. In the late 1560s, a marriage between Norfolk and Mary, Queen of Scots was mooted. Whilst it had widespread support amongst her councillors, Elizabeth was furious when she discovered the plan, and Norfolk was imprisoned. Released, he became entangled in the Ridolfi Plot to replace Elizabeth with Mary, and was executed for treason.

Howard, Lord William (c. 1510–1573) Half-brother of Thomas Howard, 3rd Duke of Norfolk, Howard was a prominent courtier throughout his life. He deputised as Earl Marshal at the coronation of his niece, Anne Boleyn, and held the canopy over Elizabeth I at her baptism. He was imprisoned, but later pardoned after the fall of Katheryn Howard, and took part in the Wars of the Rough Wooing. Supporting Mary I against Lady Jane Grey and then Wyatt, he was rewarded with the post of Lord Admiral.

James VI & I, King of Great Britain (1566–1625) Son of Mary, Queen of Scots and Henry Stuart, Lord Darnley, James became King of Scotland at just over a year old when the Scottish nobles forced his mother to abdicate. He became the first monarch of a united Scotland, England and Ireland (Great Britain) in March 1603 when Elizabeth died.

Knollys, Sir Francis (c. 1512–1596) Knollys was a member of the House of Commons in several of Henry VIII's Parliaments, and became a Gentleman Pensioner in 1539, not long before he married Katherine Carey, Elizabeth's cousin. A committed Protestant, he took his family into exile under Mary. They returned in 1559 and he was appointed to the Privy Council. Throughout Elizabeth's reign, he promoted Puritanism and a strong anti-Spanish, anti-Catholic viewpoint.

Knollys, Lettice, Countess of Leicester (1543–1634) Daughter of two of Elizabeth's favourite courtiers, Lettice had a position in the queen's household from a young age. She married the 1st Earl of Essex, by whom she had four children. In 1578, she married the Earl of Leicester in secret. Elizabeth was so hurt and outraged by the match that, although she forgave him, she refused ever to see Lettice again, relenting only once, on the urging of Lettice's son. Nevertheless, Lettice and Leicester had a happy marriage. She married a third time, to Christopher Blount, a friend of her son's.

Marie of Guise, Queen of Scots (1515–1560) A member of the powerful house of Guise-Lorraine, Marie married the Duke of Longueville, then, widowed, rejected King Henry VIII of England in favour of King James V of Scotland. She acted as regent for her daughter, Mary, Queen of Scots, but died in the middle of a war between the Protestant and Catholic factions in Scotland.

Mary I, Queen of England (1516–1558) Daughter of Henry VIII and his first wife, Katharine of Aragon, Mary became England's first queen-regnant in 1553. She sought to reinstate Catholicism following the brief reign of her Protestant half-brother, Edward VI, but died at the age of 42, after a reign of only five years, to be succeeded by Elizabeth.

Mary, Queen of Scots and Queen of France (1542–1587) Daughter of James V and Marie of Guise, Mary was six days old when her father died, and she inherited his throne. Engaged to the dauphin and sent to live at the French court at the age of five, the widowed Mary returned to Scotland 13 years later. Mary was the first queen-regnant in the British Isles and her reign was marked by religious and political rivalry between the pro-English Protestant party and the pro-French Catholic party. Mary was deposed

in 1568 and subsequently imprisoned in England until her execution in 1587 for involvement in a plot against Elizabeth.

Neville, Charles, 6th Earl of Westmorland (1542–1605) Brought up at the family seat of Raby Castle in a traditional Catholic, feudal household, resistant to the Reformation, he was a signatory to the proclamation of Mary I as queen, even though he was only eleven. His religion and his loyalty to the Crown came into conflict in the 1560s, and, somewhat reluctantly and strongly influenced by his wife, Jane Howard, he became a leading figure in the Rising of the North. After its collapse, he went into exile. The government tried to kidnap him from the Netherlands, but he avoided capture and died there.

North, Edward, 1st Baron North (c. 1504–1564) North, trained as a lawyer, became a Clerk to Parliament in 1531, and worked with members of Henry VIII's Council, including Cromwell. By 1544, he was knighted and a Chancellor to the Court of Augmentations (the body that disposed of monastic lands). He was a Privy Councillor under both Edward VI and Mary I, but although Elizabeth visited him several times, his dissent from her 1559 Act of Uniformity kept him out of government.

Parker, Matthew, Archbishop of Canterbury (1504–1575) Parker was educated at Cambridge, and took up a Fellowship at Corpus Christi during the 1520s-30s, a period of intense theological debate. He was an associate of the radical Thomas Bilney. In 1535, he was appointed chaplain to Queen Anne Boleyn, who asked him to watch over her daughter. He was elected as Archbishop of Canterbury soon after Elizabeth's succession. More radical than the queen in religion, he accepted the settlement of 1559, but hoped for further reform. He left a large quantity of medieval books and manuscripts, the Parker Library, to Corpus Christi.

Parr, Katherine, Queen of England (1512–1548) The sixth and last wife of Henry VIII, Katherine had been married and widowed twice before she married the king. She built close relationships with all three of Henry's children. She caused some scandal by marrying Sir Thomas Seymour within months of Henry's death, and there was further scandal surrounding the relationship between her young stepdaughter, Elizabeth, and her new husband. Sadly, Katherine died of puerperal fever following the birth of her first child, Mary Seymour, less than two years after the old king.

Parr, William, 1st Marquis of Northampton (1513–1571) The brother of Queen Katherine Parr, he was a staunch Protestant and a leading light in the government of Edward VI. He had a complicated private life, and his first marriage was annulled, then reinstated, then again annulled. His third wife was Helena Snakenberg, who came to the court in the train of Cecilia of Sweden. He sat on the commission that tried Thomas Howard, 4th Duke of Norfolk.

Parry, Blanche (c. 1507–1590) Blanche was the niece of Lady Troy of Herbert, principal lady-in-waiting to Elizabeth in the 1530s. Blanche joined the household early enough to rock Elizabeth's cradle, and remained at her side until her own death. When Elizabeth was queen, Blanche succeeded Mrs Astley as Chief Gentlewoman and became keeper of the queen's personal jewels. She was reputed to have an acerbic wit, but to be generous to friends and family. The altar cloth she donated to Bacton Church where she is buried has been recognised as a part of one of Elizabeth's own gowns.

Paulet, William, 1st Marquis of Winchester (c. 1475–1572) Paulet's first public position was as Sheriff of Hampshire in 1511. He worked his way through local government politics to the Privy Council by 1526 and became joint Master of King's Wards that year and later Master of the Court of Wards. By the end of Henry VIII's reign he was Lord President of the Council. He was an adherent of the Duke of Northumberland but retained a post in Mary's Council. Under Elizabeth, his lax, even fraudulent, management of the office of Lord Treasurer led to him owing a huge sum to the Crown on his death.

Perrot, Sir John (1528–1592) Perrot was educated at St David's Cathedral School and became a noted linguist, speaking English, Welsh, French, Latin, Italian and Spanish. He joined the royal household in 1532 but soon gained a reputation as quarrelsome and violent. On a diplomatic trip to France in 1551, he saved the French king from attack by a boar. He served briefly in Ireland 1571-3, then had a commission to harass Spanish shipping. In 1584-88 he was Lord Deputy of Ireland – surviving the ordeal better than most. Having quarrelled once too often, he was accused of treason and sent to the Tower. Evidence was adduced that he had referred to Elizabeth as 'a base bastard pissing kitchen woman'. He died prior to execution.

Philip II, King of Spain, Duke of Burgundy (1527–1598) Philip inherited Spain as well as the Netherlands from his father, Emperor Charles V. Whilst he eventually brought the Italian Wars to an end with the Treaty of Cateau-Cambrésis, much of his life was devoted to protecting Catholicism in Europe and trying to maintain control of the Netherlands. The Armada he sent against England in 1588 failed, undermining his control of his Spanish territories in the New World.

Radcliffe, Thomas, 3rd Earl of Essex (c. 1526–1583) His career began in Henry VIII's 1544 campaign against Boulogne, where he was knighted. Henry favoured him as a jouster, and he bore the canopy at the king's funeral. Not in favour during Edward's reign, he became a Gentleman of the Privy Chamber to King Philip and in 1556 was appointed Governor of Ireland. He retained this post under Elizabeth, being promoted to Lord Lieutenant. His animosity towards O'Neill did not improve the situation in Ireland and he was recalled. In 1568, he was appointed President of the Council of the North.

Raleigh, Sir Walter (c. 1554–1618)
Raleigh studied at Oxford and fought in
the Netherlands before taking part in an
exploratory journey to the Americas with his
half-brother, Humphrey Gilbert. Catching
Elizabeth I's eye, he became Captain of her
Guard before incurring her wrath by his
secret marriage to Elizabeth Throckmorton.
To regain favour, he set off on an expedition
to find El Dorado and sponsored two
attempts to found colonies in America. James
VI & I disliked Raleigh, and he was found
guilty of plotting the king's death. He spent
12 years in the Tower of London, working on
his *History of the World*, before being released.
Another voyage to find El Dorado failed and
he was executed for interfering with Spanish
shipping, against orders.

**Rich, Sir Richard, 1st Baron Rich (c. 1496–
1567)** Rich has probably the worst reputation
of any politician of the Tudor period
– dishonest, rapacious, double-dealing,
and a bearer of false witness. Appointed
Solicitor-General in 1533, he acted as
Cromwell's second in the Dissolution of the
Monasteries. His (probably false) testimony
was instrumental in the convictions of Sir
Thomas More and Bishop John Fisher for
treason. Rich turned against Cromwell and
became associated with the conservative
faction in religion, personally taking part in
the racking of Anne Askew. He re-emerged
as a reformer under Edward VI, whom he
served as Lord Chancellor. Under Mary he
persecuted Protestants, before going on to
advise Elizabeth during the early part of her
reign.

Robsart, Amy, Lady Dudley (1532–1560)
The daughter of a Norfolk gentleman,
Amy's marriage to Lord Robert Dudley,
son of the Duke of Northumberland, was
probably a love-match, as she was of much
lower rank than her husband. Following
Northumberland's attempt to put Lady Jane
Grey on the throne, Robert was imprisoned.
After his release, the couple lived quietly
until the accession of Elizabeth. Robert
became the queen's Master of Horse, and

it was soon rumoured that Elizabeth was
in love with him. In 1560 Amy was found
dead at the bottom of a staircase. The
circumstances of her death have never been
fully explained.

**Russell, Anne, Countess of Warwick
(c. 1548–1604)** Daughter of Francis Russell,
2nd Earl of Bedford, Anne joined the court
on Elizabeth's accession and five years later
married Ambrose, Earl of Warwick, brother
of Elizabeth I's favourite, Lord Robert
Dudley. Despite a significant age gap and the
failure of the marriage to produce children,
the couple were happy. Anne became 'more
beloved and in greater favour ... than any
other woman in the kingdom', according to
her niece, Lady Anne Clifford, and remained
with Elizabeth until the queen's death.

**Russell, John, 1st Earl of Bedford
(c. 1485–1555)** Russell began his career as
Gentleman of the Chamber to Henry VII. In
Henry VIII's reign, he was one of the circle
of jousters who surrounded the young king.
In favour with Cardinal Wolsey, he slowly
climbed to prominence, and negotiated on
behalf of the king with Pope Clement VII.
He survived Wolsey's downfall and remained
close to the king. He continued in the
Privy Council under Edward, receiving the
earldom of Bedford. He was Lord Privy Seal
under Mary and participated in her wedding
to Philip of Spain.

**Sackville, Thomas, Earl of Dorset
(c. 1536–1608)** Sackville sat in several of
Elizabeth's parliaments, but is best known
for his poetry, including partial authorship
of *Gorboduc*, the controversial play acted in
front of Elizabeth to encourage her to settle
the succession. Despite this, he gained favour
with Elizabeth, sat on her Privy Council and
was sent on embassies abroad. He was placed
under house arrest in 1587 after severely
criticising Leicester's administration in the
Netherlands. He was forgiven and appointed
as Lord Treasurer after Burghley's death.

Seymour, Edward, Duke of Somerset (c. 1500–1552) The brother of Queen Jane Seymour, he received the earldom of Hertford on the birth of his nephew, Edward. Throughout the latter years of Henry VIII's reign he was a leading councillor, and a military commander of high repute – leading the English forces against Scotland. On Henry's death, in defiance of the late king's instructions, Somerset took on the role of Lord Protector and the dukedom of Somerset. His good intentions were marred by a high-handed manner that alienated his colleagues. He was removed from office, but remained on the Council until further charges were trumped up against him and he was executed.

Seymour, Edward, Viscount Beauchamp and Earl of Hertford (1539–1621) Son of Lord Protector Somerset, he fell in love with Lady Katherine Grey, sister of the ill-fated Lady Jane. The two married in secret. When Elizabeth discovered the match, the pair were sent to the Tower. Lady Katherine bore a son, and later, a second son, after the Lieutenant of the Tower allowed them to meet. They were separated and Katherine died young. Seymour made two more clandestine matches, but was eventually received back into royal favour.

Seymour, Sir Thomas, 1st Baron of Sudeley (c. 1505–1549) Brother of Queen Jane Seymour, he was liked by Henry VIII, but given little influence. On the king's death, he was appointed Lord High Admiral, but resented his brother's position as Lord Protector. He secretly married the dowager-queen, Katherine Parr. His inappropriate behaviour with 14-year-old Elizabeth, and his attempts to marry her after being widowed, contributed to the charges of treason that ended with his execution.

Shelton, Mary, Lady Scudamore (c. 1550–1603) A Boleyn connection of Elizabeth's, she became a chamberer in 1571 and was soon one of the queen's three favourite sleeping companions. When Mary married Sir John Scudamore without asking royal consent, the queen reacted angrily, apparently breaking Mary's finger by throwing a brush at her. Nevertheless, the storm blew over, and Mary was seen as a particularly effective intermediary with the queen – a position from which she benefited financially.

Sidney, Sir Henry (1529–1586) Sidney was brought up in the household of Edward VI and was knighted in 1551. An adherent of Northumberland, he married the duke's daughter, Mary. He was speedily forgiven for his involvement with the Lady Jane Grey affair, and gained favour with King Philip, who stood godson to Sidney's son, Philip. In Elizabeth's reign, he benefited from being the brother-in-law of Lord Robert Dudley and was appointed as President of the Council of Wales, and twice as Lord Lieutenant of Ireland.

Sidney, Sir Philip (1554–1586) The nephew of Elizabeth's favourite, Robert Dudley, Earl of Leicester, Philip won praise for his intellect and his ability – although he displeased the queen when he criticised her proposed marriage to the Duke of Anjou. His most famous works are *The Countess of Pembroke's Arcadia*, dedicated to his sister, and the *Stella and Astrophel* sonnets, which took Lady Penelope Devereux as his muse. A committed Protestant, he urged English support for the Protestant insurgents in the Netherlands and died from wounds sustained at the Battle of Zutphen.

Southwell, Sir Richard (c. 1503–1564) Southwell first entered royal circles as tutor to Gregory Cromwell, son of Thomas. Subsequently, he served Henry VIII, Edward VI, Mary I and Elizabeth I in various roles – Privy Councillor, High Sheriff of Norfolk and Suffolk, and Master of the Armoury.

Spenser, Edmund (c. 1552–1599) A graduate of Pembroke College, Cambridge, Spenser served in Elizabeth's army in Ireland. Like many Elizabethans, he advocated total domination of Ireland, and lost his own home there during the war. Spenser wrote some of the most admired poems and prose in English, including *The Faerie Queen*, developing his own rhyming scheme. Elizabeth admired his verse, and paid him a pension.

Squire, Edward (d. 1598) In 1595, Squire sailed in the *Frances*, amongst Drake's squadron to the Americas. Separated from the rest of the fleet, the *Frances* was taken to Seville, where Squire was allegedly converted by the Jesuits. He was later accused of attempting to poison both Elizabeth and Essex. He confessed under torture and was hanged, drawn and quartered, but the evidence suggests the accusations were, if not entirely falsified, certainly exaggerated.

Stanley, Henry, 4th Earl of Derby (1531–1593) Connected to much of the English nobility, Stanley was married to Lady Margaret Clifford, daughter of Henry VIII's niece, Lady Eleanor Brandon. A Privy Councillor to Elizabeth and her ambassador to France, he took part in the trial of Mary, Queen of Scots, and later acted as Lord High Steward at the trial of Philip Howard, Earl of Arundel.

Stuart, Lady Arbella (1575–1615) Arbella was the great-great-granddaughter of Henry VII, and paternal first cousin to James VI of Scotland. Her parents had married without royal permission, but Elizabeth was persuaded to forgive them. Arbella was orphaned as an infant and brought up first by her paternal grandmother, Lady Lennox, then by her maternal one, Lady Shrewsbury, who hoped she would be named the queen's heir. She was treated with suspicion by Elizabeth, and forced to remain under virtual house arrest. Life improved under James VI & I but a secret marriage to William Seymour ended with imprisonment and her death from a long decline after she refused to eat.

Talbot, George, 6th Earl of Shrewsbury (c. 1522–1590) Shrewsbury had an impressive early career, and by 1565 was joint Lieutenant-General of the North. Widowed with seven children, he married Elizabeth Hardwick as her fourth husband, with a complex financial settlement, including cross-marriages between their children. Their happy domestic life was turned upside down when Elizabeth appointed Shrewsbury as the 'guardian' of Mary, Queen of Scots. The stress and expense of this role ruined his marriage, his finances, his health, and his relationship with his heir, Gilbert.

Tallis, Thomas (c. 1505–1585) Tallis is first found as organist at the Benedictine Priory of Dover in 1535, and later at the Augustinian Prior at Waltham Abbey. When this was dissolved he received a pension and moved to Canterbury Cathedral. By 1544 he was a member of the Chapel Royal and continued in it until his death. He composed extensively for the Chapel, his most complex work being *Gaude gloriosa Dei mater*. His works continue to be performed in Anglican services.

Throckmorton, Elizabeth (Bess), Lady Raleigh (1565–c. 1647) Daughter of Sir Nicholas, Elizabeth I's ambassador to Mary, Queen of Scots, Bess joined the court as a Gentlewoman of the Privy Chamber. She and Sir Walter Raleigh fell in love and married without royal permission. The furious queen imprisoned them both, but had no grounds for her action, as neither had royal blood, so did not need her consent for their union. Sir Walter was eventually forgiven, but Bess did not re-join the court. After Raleigh's execution, it is claimed Bess kept his head in a silken bag.

Walsingham, Sir Francis (c 1532–1590) Walsingham was a firm Protestant. He was Elizabeth's ambassador to France, where he witnessed the Massacre of St Bartholomew's Day, which convinced him that Elizabeth and England were vulnerable to Catholic plotting. Working with Lord Burghley, he set up a comprehensive espionage system which concentrated on identifying Catholic plotters. His patient work led to the uncovering of the Babington Plot to replace Elizabeth with Mary, Queen of Scots – although he probably had a hand in inciting the conspiracy.

Wharton, Thomas, 2nd Baron Wharton (1520–1572) Like his father and grandfather, Wharton's career was centred on military service on the Anglo-Scottish Border. He was knighted by Somerset in 1545, after taking part in an invasion of Scotland. Wharton remained a Catholic, consequently his career flagged under Edward but burgeoned under Mary. He was a witness to her will and took part in her funeral. Under Elizabeth, his religion was a bar to progress, and he spent several weeks in the Tower. He did little to impede the Rising of the North, but was saved from punishment by a life-threatening injury.

Wriothesley, Henry, 2nd Earl of Southampton (1545–1581) Henry lost his father young, and although his wardship was granted to William Herbert, Earl of Pembroke, he was brought up by his mother, Jane, who maintained the Catholic faith. Henry married the Catholic Mary Browne, and during Elizabeth's reign was suspected of plotting with Mary, Queen of Scots and the Spanish ambassador. He returned to favour after a spell in the Tower, but died young, estranged from his wife.

Wriothesley, Henry, 3rd Earl of Southampton (1573–1624) Only six when his father died, his wardship and marriage was granted to Lord Burghley. On reaching his majority, he refused Burghley's choice of a bride, and was obliged to pay his guardian £5,000. Southampton appears to have been bisexual, close to several men who remained unmarried. He did, however, attract royal wrath for impregnating one of the queen's ladies and refusing to marry her. He was a patron of literature, including Shakespeare. He joined the faction of the Earl of Essex and was condemned for treason after supporting Essex's failed rebellion. On Elizabeth's death, he was released from the Tower and became highly influential in the reign of James VI & I.

Wyatt the Younger, Thomas (1521–1554) Son of the poet, Wyatt the Younger was a firm Protestant and led a rebellion against Mary I. His stated aim was to prevent the queen's marriage to Philip of Spain, but Mary and her government believed he planned to overthrow the queen and replace her with her half-sister, Elizabeth. Wyatt was executed, having exonerated Elizabeth of any involvement.

INDEX OF EVENTS

A short description of events that are not self-explanatory.

January

• In exchange for English support against the Duke of Guise and the Catholic League, the Huguenots of France promised that the port of Newhaven/Le Havre would be given to England as security until the French Crown had been forced to return the formerly English town of Calais. The plan failed.

• Norfolk had planned to marry Mary, Queen of Scots – a scheme which had the support of much of Elizabeth's Council, but which no one had the courage to broach with her. Initially pardoned, Norfolk was eventually executed for treason, following involvement in the Ridolfi plot to free the Scottish queen.

February

• Robert Devereux, 2nd Earl of Essex, was the last of Elizabeth's favourites, and she consistently promoted him, including to the lieutenancy of Ireland. His arrogance, general recklessness and occasional insolence to the queen made him many enemies. When she punished him for deserting his post in Ireland, he mounted a rebellion that ended in ignominious failure.

• In the wake of Wyatt's Rebellion in 1554, Elizabeth was summoned to Whitehall, having previously refused to come to her half-sister's court on a plea of sickness. There was some evidence implicating her in the revolt, and she was sent to the Tower. However, charges could not be substantiated and she was released to house arrest.

March

• During her reign, Elizabeth tried to balance supporting her Protestant co-religionists in the Netherlands in their fight for independence against their feudal overlord, Philip of Spain, with her reluctance to see

sovereigns undermined in their own realms. Depending on the turn of political events she sometimes proffered help, and other times appeared unwilling to intervene.

April

• The Peace of Cateau-Cambrésis finally ended the war that had been waged between France and Spain for dominance in Italy since 1494. Unfortunately, Elizabeth's alliance with Spain was not strong enough for the return of Calais (lost during the final phase of the war) to be one of the clauses.

May

• The Council of Trent first opened in 1545 with a view to bridging the ever-widening gap between the Catholic Church and the Reformers, who were by that time coalescing into different Protestant groups. It failed to achieve its original mission, but instituted the Counter-Reformation, that is, the invigoration of the Catholic Church.

June

• Rodrigo Lopez was a Portuguese Jew, who became Elizabeth's physician in 1586. He was accused by the Earl of Essex of being in league with two men accused of being Spanish spies. Although Lord Burghley thought Lopez innocent, Essex had him taken to the Tower, and rejecting Lopez' defence of employment by Sir Francis Walsingham, ensured he was convicted of conspiring to poison the queen.

July

• Edward VI attempted to change the succession as enacted in the 1544 Act of Succession. He excluded his half-sisters, Mary and Elizabeth, and nominated his cousin, Lady Jane Grey. After his death,

Jane's father-in-law attempted to implement this but public opinion was against it and Mary was widely supported. Elizabeth remained quietly in the country, declining to involve herself.

August

• Although the Armada of 1588 had been defeated, hostilities with Spain continued, and in 1594, the Spanish landed at Mount's Bay in Cornwall, sacking Newlyn, Penzance, Mousehole and Paul. The local militia was defeated, but a larger defence force was gathered and the Spanish withdrew.

• In 1595, the Irish, led by Hugh O'Neill rose up against the increasingly hated English domination. The issue of religion had exacerbated the long-standing resentment of an occupying force. In the summer of 1598 O'Neill besieged the fort at Blackwater, then ambushed and wiped out the relieving force under Henry Bagenal at Yellow Ford.

• Sir Francis Throckmorton, Catholic nephew of one of Elizabeth's ambassadors, became embroiled in a plot to free Mary, Queen of Scots. After having him watched for months, Walsingham instigated a raid on his house, and incriminating evidence, including lists of ports suitable for an invading fleet, was found. Throckmorton confessed after being racked, and was executed.

• During his reign, Ivan IV (the Terrible), Tsar of Russia endeavoured to promote both trading and military links with England. He corresponded with Elizabeth, and sent ambassadors, including Andrea Andrea Gregorovich Saviena. Elizabeth agreed that, should the need arise, Ivan could take refuge in England – provided he paid his own expenses.

September

• As the war in the Netherlands intensified, Elizabeth was finally persuaded to send English troops. Amongst them was Sir Philip Sidney, a rising star at her court, a poet, and a committed Protestant. The English troops, led by Sidney's uncle, besieged the town of Zutphen. An ambush was laid to prevent the Spanish, sending in supplies. Sidney was seriously wounded and died a few weeks later.

• Princess Cecilia was the beautiful, and scandal-beset, daughter of Gustav Vasa I of Sweden. She corresponded with Elizabeth for some years, and following her marriage to the Margrave of Baden-Rodemachen, visited the English court. The royal ladies formed a friendship, and Cecilia remained for some months, bearing her first child in England.

October

• John Somerville, of Warwickshire, was arrested when he announced that he was on his way to London to shoot the queen. He was probably not of sound mind, but both he and his father-in-law, Edward Arden were executed. The government's reaction was forceful, partly in reaction to the recent assassination of William the Silent, Prince of Orange.

November

• Elizabeth's open flirtation with the married Lord Robert Dudley had already caused tensions. When his wife died in mysterious circumstances, Mary, Queen of Scots and France was heard to announce that Elizabeth 'intend(ed) to marry her horse-keeper, who has murdered his wife to make room for her.' Mary's scorn would later come back to haunt her.

December

• Following the Battle of the Yellow Ford, and the failure of Essex' lieutenancy, Lord Mountjoy was appointed to command the English forces in Ireland against O'Neill. The Spanish supported their co-religionists and landed an army at Kinsale. The town was besieged, and, when O'Neill attempted to relieve it, Mountjoy cut his army to pieces.

Queen Elizabeth I Book of Days
Published in Great Britain in 2021 by
Graffeg Limited.

Written by Tudor Times
Designed and produced by Graffeg Limited
copyright © 2021.

Tudor Times Ltd
www.tudortimes.co.uk

Graffeg Limited, 24 Stradey Park Business
Centre, Mwrwg Road, Llangennech,
Llanelli, Carmarthenshire, SA14 8YP,
Wales, UK. Tel: 01554 824000.
www.graffeg.com.

Tudor Times is hereby identified as the
author of this work in accordance with
section 77 of the Copyrights, Designs and
Patents Act 1988.

A CIP Catalogue record for this book is
available from the British Library.

ISBN 9781913134860

1 2 3 4 5 6 7 8 9

FSC www.fsc.org

MIX
Paper from
responsible sources
FSC® C014138

Photo credits:

Cover image: Queen Elizabeth I, 'The
Ermine Portrait', Nicholas Hilliard,
1585, from the Elizabeth I and her People
exhibition at the National Portrait Gallery
Photo reproduced by permission of the
Marquess of Salisbury, Hatfield House.

Page 3, 4, 9, 19: Folger Shakespeare Library
Collection.